City & Guilds

Level 1 Certificate for IT Users

Presentation Graphics

Level
1

marie Wyatt

City&
Guilds

 Heinemann

Heinemann Educational Publishers
Halley Court, Jordan Hill, Oxford, OX2 8EJ
Part of Harcourt Education

Heinemann is the registered trademark of Harcourt Education Ltd

First published in 2002
2005 2004 2003
10 9 8 7 6 5 4 3 2

A catalogue record for this book is available from the British Library on request.

ISBN 0 435 46265 2

Typeset by Techset Ltd, Gateshead
Printed and bound in UK by Thomson Litho Ltd

Tel: 01865 888058 www.heinemann.co.uk

Contents

1127512

Introduction

City & Guilds e-Quals is an exciting new range of IT qualifications developed with leading industry experts. These comprehensive, progressive awards cover everything from getting to grips with basic IT to gaining the latest professional skills.

The range consists of both user and practitioner qualifications. User qualifications (Levels 1–3) are ideal for those who use IT as part of their job or in life generally, while Practitioner qualifications (Levels 2–3) have been developed for those who need to boost their professional skills in, for example, networking or software development.

e-Quals boasts on-line testing and a dedicated website with news and support materials and web-based training. The qualifications reflect industry standards and meet the requirements of the National Qualifications Framework.

With e-Quals you will not only develop your expertise, you will gain a qualification that is recognised by employers all over the world.

This book assumes the use of Microsoft PowerPoint 2000 and is for beginners who have a basic knowledge of the mouse and keyboard. The purpose of presentation graphics software is to enable you to present and communicate information. PowerPoint makes it easy to design professional-looking presentations incorporating text and graphics, which can be used to run as slideshows on a computer or used as handouts or overhead transparencies.

The unit is organised into 4 outcomes. You will learn to:

- Create and edit presentations text
- Create and edit presentations graphics
- Position and manipulate text and graphics
- Create, print and demonstrate a multi-slide show.

This book covers the specific skills and underpinning knowledge for the outcomes of the Presentation Graphics unit although they are not dealt with separately or in this order.

Each section covers several practical features as well as underpinning knowledge related to the unit outcomes. This is followed by skills practice and a chance to check your knowledge. Consolidation tasks give you the opportunity to put together skills and knowledge, and practice assignments complete your progress towards the actual assignment. As with all skills, practise makes perfect! Solutions to the skills practice, knowledge checks, consolidation and practice assignments can be found at the back of the book.

Your tutor will give you a copy of the outcomes, as provided by City & Guilds, so that you can sign and date each learning point as you master the skills and knowledge.

There is often more than one way of carrying out a task in PowerPoint, e.g. using the toolbar, menu or keyboard. Whilst this book may use one method, there are others, and alternatives are listed at the back in the quick reference guide.

The tasks are designed to be worked through in order, as earlier tasks may be used in later sections. Good luck!

You will learn to

- Load PowerPoint
- Identify parts of the PowerPoint window
- Create a new presentation
- Choose slide layouts
- Enter text onto slides
- Save a presentation
- Review slides
- Close a presentation
- Close PowerPoint
- Close down the computer

This section introduces to you the PowerPoint environment. Here you will create your first presentation of several slides and learn how to review and save your presentation.

Information: Using the mouse

The following are terms used to describe mouse actions used in this book:

Click   Press the left mouse button and release
Double click   Press the left mouse button and release, twice, in quick succession
Drag   Hold the left button down and move the mouse. Release the mouse button.

Task 1.1   Load PowerPoint

Method

1   Switch on your computer.
2   If you are using a network you will need a User ID and a password to log on. Check with your tutor.
3   Wait for the Windows desktop to appear.
4   Move the mouse pointer over the **Start** button on the **taskbar** and click the left mouse button – a menu appears (Figure 1.1). Your menus may look slightly different to this depending on the programs available to you.
5   Move the mouse up the menu and point to **Programs** – another menu appears to the right.
6   Move the mouse to **Microsoft PowerPoint** and click the left button to load. (Depending on your computer setup, you may have to click on Office 2000 first.)
7   The **PowerPoint** opening dialogue box should appear (Figure 1.2).

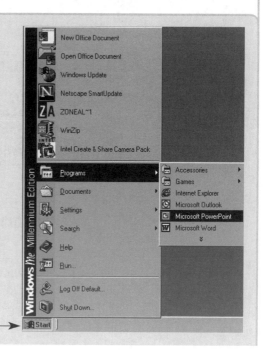

Figure 1.1 Loading PowerPoint

Start ⟶ 🏁Start

Alternatively, you may have a PowerPoint icon 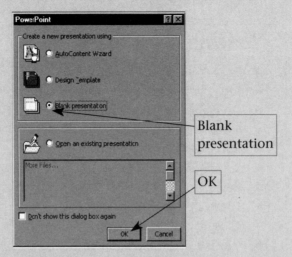 on your desktop.

Double click the left mouse button to load PowerPoint.

Figure 1.2 Opening dialogue box

8   Click on **Blank presentation** option.

9   Click on **OK**. New Slide Layout dialogue box appears (Figure 1.3).

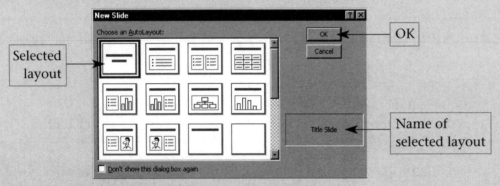

Figure 1.3 New Slide AutoLayouts

10   Click **OK**. PowerPoint's Normal view appears (Figure 1.4).

Information

Each PowerPoint 'page' is called a slide. There are many slide **AutoLayouts** or templates to choose from which help you set out the presentation in a consistent manner. The first layout – the Title Slide – is a good choice for the first slide of a new presentation.

Information: Identify parts of the PowerPoint Tri-Pane window

The window is divided into three panes – **Slide**, **Outline** and **Notes**. You will work in the Slide and Outline panes.

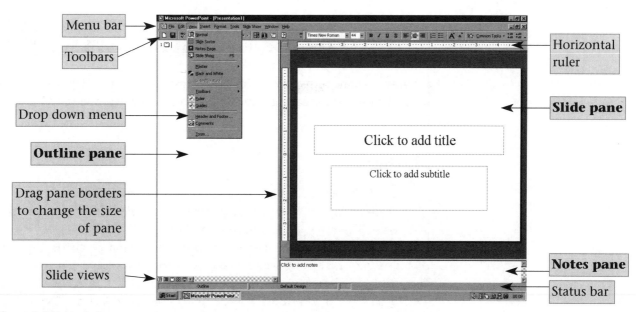

Figure 1.4 Normal view

Labels (clockwise from top left):
- Menu bar
- Toolbars
- Drop down menu
- Outline pane
- Drag pane borders to change the size of pane
- Slide views
- Horizontal ruler
- Slide pane
- Notes pane
- Status bar

Slide content: Click to add title / Click to add subtitle / Click to add notes

- **Title bar** Displays the name of the current presentation. The default (or automatic) filename is **Presentation 1**.
- **Menu bar** Menus can be selected by using the mouse or keyboard. Each menu drops down to give further options. Initially a list of basic options appears followed a few seconds later by a full list. This list will change according to the items you have most recently selected. You can click on ⚯ at the bottom of a menu to expand the list of options.
- **Toolbar** Features shortcut buttons for frequently used actions such as Save. If you position the mouse over a button and wait, a **Screen Tip** will appear giving an explanation of its function (Figure 1.5).

Standard toolbar   Formatting toolbar

Figure 1.5 Toolbars

The **Standard toolbar** is, by default, combined with the **Formatting toolbar**, which is used for changing the appearance of objects, e.g. making text bold. Both of these toolbars hold the more frequently used buttons but

can be expanded to show more by clicking on **More Buttons**

- **Horizontal ruler** This aids accurate placement of objects on the page. There is also a **Vertical ruler** down the left side of the Slide pane. If not visible, select **Ruler** from the **View** menu.
- **Status bar** When working on slides, the status bar displays the number of slides, e.g. Slide 1 of 4.
- **Slide view** icons These allow different methods of viewing the presentation. All views can also be accessed via the **View** menu except Slide view.

Task 1.2 | Displaying different slide views

The current (default) display is **Normal view** as shown in Figure 1.4. This view can be used for creating and editing slides. Try other views as shown in Figure 1.6.

Method

1   Click on **Outline** view. This view displays an outline of the presentation showing text only. Text can be entered or edited in this view. The other panes are reduced in size.
2   Click on **Slide** view. This view displays the slide itself and is used for creating and editing slides. The other panes are reduced in size.
3   Click on **Slide Sorter** view. This view provides an overview of all slides in miniature (you currently only have one) and can be used for changing the order of slides and deleting slides.
4   Click on **Slide Show** view. This is used for viewing each slide on a full screen. As there is nothing to view yet, press **Esc** (top left of keyboard).

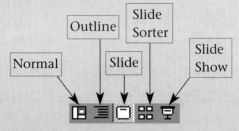

Figure 1.6 Slide views

Information

Placeholders are automatically displayed on new slides chosen from Slide AutoLayouts, ready for you to enter text, graphics or other objects. In Figure 1.7 they are text placeholders. Placeholders themselves do not show in your final presentation nor do they print. They are formatted automatically to a particular font and size and this ensures consistent presentation from one slide to another. If the text you need to key in is longer (wider) than the placeholder, the text will wrap onto the next line. A red wavy line may appear under some text as you key it in. Ignore this for now – it means that the word is spelt incorrectly or it is not in the dictionary. You will learn about the spellcheck later.

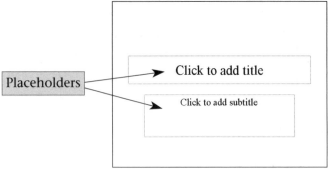

Figure 1.7 Placeholders

Hint:

Make sure your monitor is tilted to a position that is comfortable for you.

Task 1.3 — Entering text onto a slide

Method

1. Click in the top placeholder (**Click to add title**). The black vertical flashing line is the cursor where text will appear when keyed in. Key in your name.
2. Click in the second placeholder (**Click to add subtitle**) and key in **My First Presentation**.

Task 1.4 — Create a new slide

Method

1. Click on **New Slide** button on the Standard toolbar. If it is not visible click on More buttons and select (it should then remain visible on the toolbar).
2. Click on the second Slide Layout **Bulleted List**.
3. Click in top placeholder (**Click to add title**) and key in **PowerPoint**.
4. Click in lower placeholder (**Click to add text**). Key in **Present information**. Press **Enter**.
5. Another bullet appears. Key in **Add text**. Press **Enter**.
6. Another bullet appears. Key in **Add graphics**.

Hint:

In a bulleted list, each time you press Enter a new bullet appears. If you have pressed Enter after the last item, click on the Bullets button to remove the unwanted bullet.

Information

Bullet points are used to itemise a list of key points to make them stand out.

Task 1.5 — Create a further new slide

Method

1. Click on **New Slide** button on the Standard toolbar.
2. Click on the second Slide Layout **Bulleted List**.
3. Click in top placeholder (**Click to add title**) and key in **Different Views**.
4. Click in lower placeholder (**Click to add text**). Key in **Normal**. Press **Enter**.
5. Another bullet appears. Key in **Outline**. Press **Enter**.
6. Another bullet appears. Key in **Slide**. Press **Enter**.
7. Another bullet appears. Key in **Slide Sorter**.

Hint:

You can also insert a **New Slide** by selecting New Slide from the **Insert** menu.

Task 1.6 — Save the presentation

When saving a presentation, all the slides are saved together as one file. Always use a filename that reflects the contents so you can identify it later. Filenames can comprise of upper or lower case letters, numbers or other characters except / \ > < * ? " | : ;

Method

1   Click on the **Save** button 🖫
2   The **Save As** dialogue box appears (Figure 1.8).
    The **Save in** box indicates where the file will be saved. By default this will be to My Documents or My Work, or to an area of a network assigned to you.

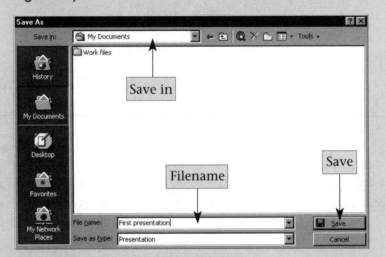

Figure 1.8 Save

3   Click in the **File name** box. Notice that the first few words of the file appear as a suggested name. Delete this by pressing **Delete** (Figure 1.9) and key in **First presentation** as the filename.

Figure 1.9 Delete

4   Click on **Save**.
    Notice how the filename appears in the blue **title bar** at the top of the window.
    View the slideshow using the different view options as you did in Task 1.2. Finish with **Slide view**.

Information: Reviewing slides

When you are working on a presentation you will want to view each slide separately to review it.

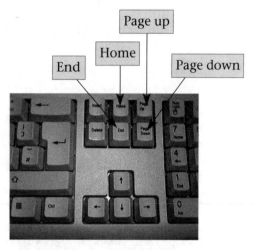

Figure 1.10 Moving around

- **Using the keyboard**
  Press **Page Up** key to display **previous** slide (Figure 1.10).
  Press **Page Down** key to display **next** slide.
  Press **Home** key to display **first** slide.
  Press **End** key to display **last** slide.

  Try each of these keys now.

- **Using the scroll bar**
  Use the vertical scroll bar on the right of the window (Figure 1.11).

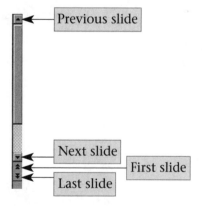

Figure 1.11 Save

Click on the appropriate **single** arrow to move to **previous** or **next** slide.

Click on the **double** arrows to move to the **first** or **last** slide.

Try each of these now.

Task 1.7　Close the file

Method

Click on the **File** menu – select **Close**. (If prompted to save, click on **Yes**.)

Task 1.8　Open a new presentation, enter text, save and close

Method

Hint:

Adjust your chair to ensure your back is supported.

1　Click on the **New** presentation button
2　Select a title slide and key in **Working with Computers** as a title.
3　Key in **Health and Safety** as a subtitle.
4　Click on **New Slide** button on the Standard toolbar.
5　Click on the second Layout slide – **Bulleted List**.
6　Click in top placeholder (**Click to add title**) and key in **Problem areas**.
7　Click in lower placeholder (**Click to add text**). Key in **Eye Strain**. Press **Enter**.
8　Another bullet appears. Key in **Back problems**. Press Enter.
9　Another bullet appears. Key in **Repetitive Strain Injury (RSI)**.
10　Save the presentation as **Health and Safety**.
11　Close the presentation.

Remember:

If you have pressed Enter after the last item, click on the Bullets button to remove the unwanted bullet.

Task 1.9　Close Powerpoint

Method

Click on **File** menu – select **Exit**.

Method

1   On a home or standalone computer, click on **Start** menu (Figure 1.12).
2   Select **Shut Down**.
3   Click on **OK** if dialogue box reads Shut down as in Figure 1.13. If not click on down arrow and select **Shut down** from list.
4   Switch off.

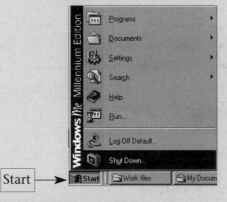

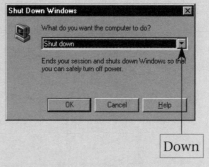

Figure 1.12 Start – Shutdown   **Figure 1.13** Shut down

On a network computer you must **log off**. Check with your supervisor/tutor. Make a note of what you have to do.

→ Practise your skills 1

1   Load PowerPoint and a new blank presentation.
2   Choose a Title slide and enter the following title: **Portway Homes**.
3   Enter the following subtitle: **Builders of Fine Homes**.
4   Insert a new slide – a bulleted list – and enter the following title: **Current locations**.
5   Enter the following list:

   ● **Wheatcroft**
   ● **Riverside Farm**
   ● **Livingstone Park**
   ● **Thames Way**

6   Insert a new slide – a bulleted list – and enter the following title: **House types**.
7   Enter the following list:

   ● **1 bedroom apartments**
   ● **2 bedroom houses**
   ● **3 bedroom semi-detached houses**
   ● **4 bedroom executive detached houses**

8   Review the slides.
9   Save the presentation as **Portway Homes**.
10   Close the presentation.

→ Practise your skills 2

1 Load PowerPoint if not already loaded and a new blank presentation.

2 Choose a Title slide and enter the following title: **Greenfingers**.

3 Enter the following subtitle: **Garden Centre**.

4 Insert a new slide – a bulleted list – and enter the following title: **Suppliers of**.

5 Enter the following list:

- **Bedding Plants**
- **Perennials**
- **Shrubs**
- **Specimen trees**
- **House plants**

6 Insert a new slide – a bulleted list – and enter the following title: **Garden Supplies**.

7 Enter the following list:

- **Peat**
- **Potting Compost**
- **Fertilizer**
- **Eco-friendly pesticides**

8 Review the slides.

9 Save the presentation as **Greenfingers**.

10 Close the presentation.

→ Check your knowledge

1 What is each PowerPoint page called?

2 The PowerPoint window is divided into three panes. What are they?

3 What should you remember when naming a presentation file?

4 What is a placeholder?

5 What are Slide AutoLayouts and what is the advantage of using them?

6 What is the purpose of using bullet points.

You will learn to

- Open an existing presentation
- Use Outline pane
- Edit text
- Quick save a presentation
- Use Undo and Redo
- Use the spellcheck

In this section you will find out how to move around a presentation and make changes to the content. Making changes to content is known as editing.

Task 2.1 | Open an existing presentation

Method

1 Click on **Open** button 📂. Open dialogue box appears (Figure 2.1).

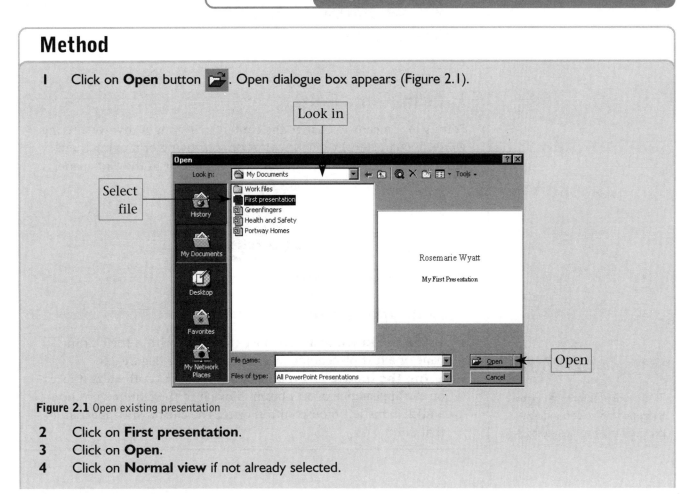

Figure 2.1 Open existing presentation

2 Click on **First presentation**.
3 Click on **Open**.
4 Click on **Normal view** if not already selected.

Hint:

You can double click on a presentation name to open it.

Another way of moving around a presentation is to click on the required slide in the Outline pane (Figure 2.2). Try this now. Move through the slides ending on the first slide.

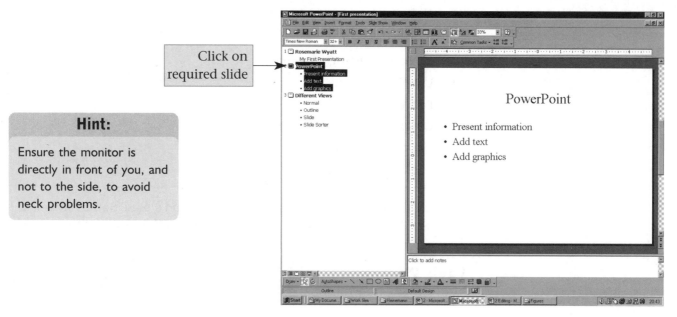

Click on required slide

Figure 2.2 Select slide using Outline pane

Information: Editing text

Editing text means to change the content. This might involve altering words or characters by deleting, inserting, copying or moving them around. Text can be edited in the Outline pane or in the Slide pane.

Figure 2.3 Keys for moving around

Moving the cursor

- **Using the keyboard** To move the cursor within the Outline pane or a text placeholder, use the arrow keys (Figure 2.3).
- **Using the mouse** As you move the mouse over the text it takes on the appearance of an I-beam. Move it to the required position and click the left mouse button once. The cursor will appear at that point.

Task 2.2   Insert text

Method

1. Using the Outline pane, on the first slide click directly in front of the word **Presentation** in the subtitle so the cursor appears, and key in **PowerPoint**. Press the spacebar once to leave a space.
2. Move to the second slide.
3. Click directly after the word **graphics** and press **Enter** to create a new bullet point.
4. Key in **Add clip art**.
5. Move to the third slide.
6. Click directly in front of the word **Views** in the title.
7. Key in the word **Slide** and press the space bar.

Task 2.3   Delete text

Characters and spaces can be deleted to the left of the cursor position or to the right.

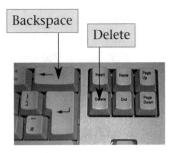

Figure 2.4 Backspace and delete

- **To delete to the left of the cursor**   Press the backspace key (Figure 2.4).
- **To delete to the right of the cursor**   Press the **Delete** key.

Method

1. Move to the first slide.
2. Click directly in front of the word **My** and press **Delete** key until the words **My First** and the following space are deleted.
3. Move to the last slide and click directly in front of the word **Slide** in the title.
4. Press **Backspace** key to delete the word **Different**.

Task 2.4   Quick save a presentation

Once a presentation has been saved and named, click on the **Save** button ![disk] to resave it at any time. Any amendments are saved overwriting the original presentation. It is good practice to save your work every ten minutes using this method in case a system error or power failure occurs. You would then only lose work up to your last save.

Method

Click on the **Save** button ![disk]

Task 2.5   Use Undo and Redo

Everybody makes mistakes sometimes. You may, for example, delete some text and then change your mind. PowerPoint has a very useful feature that remembers the last few changes you made and allows you to reverse them. It will let you **undo** a change ... and also allow you to **redo** it! Each time you click on Undo it will take you back one more stage (Figure 2.5). Clicking on the down arrow at the side of the Undo button allows you to select a particular action, but beware as it takes you back to that stage in the presentation when you performed it.

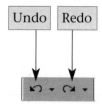

Figure 2.5 Undo and Redo

Method

I	Delete any word in the presentation.
2	Click on **Undo** – the action is undone and the word reappears.
3	Click on **Redo** – the word is deleted again.
4	Close the file. When prompted to save, select **No**.

Information: Spellchecking

PowerPoint has an automatic spellcheck that checks each word of your document against an in-built dictionary. As you enter text, any word it does not recognise will appear on screen with a red wavy line underneath, e.g. your own name. This does not necessarily mean that it is wrong but the spellcheck does not recognise it. The word may not be in the dictionary or it may be a proper name. Do not totally rely on the spellcheck as it does not spot words that are correctly spelt but used in the wrong context, e.g. I am going <u>four</u> a walk, or I am going <u>two</u> go with <u>ewe</u>. It does not check whether your sentences make sense either or whether they convey the right meaning. Use the spellcheck but always read through your presentation carefully too. This is called proofreading.

Method

1 Click on **Open** button
2 Click on **Portway Homes**.
3 Click on **Open**.
4 Select **Normal view** if not already selected.
5 Click on the Spelling and Grammar button
6 The Spelling and Grammar dialogue box appears (Figure 2.6) unless you have no errors!

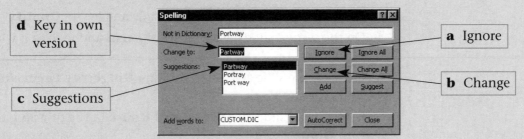

Figure 2.6 Spellcheck

7 The spellchecker scans through the presentation, stopping at any words it does not recognise and displays them in red in the spellcheck window.
8 Either:
   a Click on **Ignore** if you are satisfied with the spelling or
   b Click on **Change** to accept the highlighted suggested spelling or
   c Click on a **Suggestion** in the list and then click on **Change** or
   d Key in your own version of the word and click on **Change**.
9 The first word highlighted is **Portway**. Click **Ignore**.
10 The spellcheck continues through the presentation repeating the process. When it has finished, a message confirms the spellcheck is complete. Click **OK**.
11 Save the presentation and close.

If you had no errors, return to this section when you next need to use the spellcheck.

Hint:

It is also possible to **Add** words to the dictionary that you use frequently, such as proper names.

From now on you should always use the spellcheck and proofread your work.

Method

1 Open **Greenfingers**.
2 Click directly in front of the word **Garden**, key in **Your Local** and press the space bar.
3 Move to the second slide, delete the word **Suppliers** and key in **Stockists**.
4 Click directly after **trees** and press **Enter**.
5 Key in **Fruit trees** as the next bulleted item.

6	Move to the last slide, delete the word **Garden** in the title and key in **Sundry**.
7	Click directly after **pesticides** and press **Enter**.
8	Key in **Garden tools** as the next bulleted item.
9	Click on the **Save** button 🖫
10	Spellcheck the presentation.
11	Save and close the presentation.

→ Practise your skills 1

1 Open the existing presentation **Portway Homes**.

2 Delete the word **Fine** on the first slide and key in **Quality**.

3 On the second slide delete the word **Farm** and replace it with **Court**.

4 On the same slide add a new location **Ridgeway Farm** after **Livingstone Park**.

5 On the third slide, delete the word **House** in the title and replace with **Home**.

6 Spellcheck, save and close.

→ Practise your skills 2

1 Open the presentation **Health and Safety**.

2 On the first slide, after the word **Safety**, key in **Issues**.

3 In the title on slide 2, insert the word **Everyday** in front of **Problem**.

4 Delete the small **a** of **areas** and insert a capital **A**.

5 On the same slide change **Back** to **Muscular**.

6 Spellcheck, save and close.

Remember:

Did you spellcheck and proofread your work?

→ Check your knowledge

1 How often should you save a presentation and why?

2 You should always spellcheck your work but why should you not rely on the spellcheck alone?

3 What is this icon used for? 📂

4 What is this icon used for? 🖫

5 Text can be edited in two different panes. What are they?

Formatting text

You will learn to

- Select text
- Consider text presentation
- Format text
- Use Save As
- Print

In this section you will be formatting text. This means to alter its appearance, for example by changing its size or style.

Information

There are many ways of altering the appearance of a presentation. This is often carried out by changing selected areas of text. It is therefore useful to look at ways of selecting text before going any further. When text is selected it appears to be highlighted (white text on a black background).

To select:	Method
One word	Double click on word (also selects the following space)
Several words	Press and drag the I-beam across several words and release (Figure 3.1)
A block of text	Click cursor at start point, hold down **Shift**. Click cursor at end point.
To deselect	Click anywhere off the text

Task 3.1 Select text

Method

1 Open the presentation **Greenfingers**.
2 Move to the last slide.
3 Position cursor directly in front of **Eco-friendly** in either the Outline or the Slide pane.
4 Hold down the left mouse button and drag the I-beam across the hyphenated words and the following space. The text appears to be highlighted (Figure 3.1).
5 Click anywhere off the text to deselect.
6 Double click on the word **Fertilizers**.
7 Click anywhere off the text to deselect.

- Fertilizers
- Eco-friendly pesticides
- Garden tools

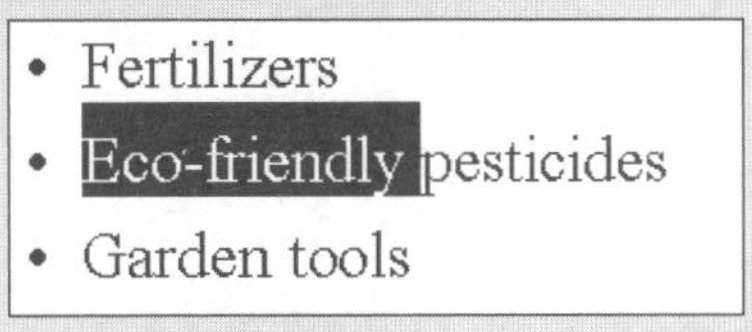

Figure 3.1 Select text

Text presentation

The purpose of a PowerPoint presentation is to get a message across to an audience. The following should be considered when preparing one:

Hint:

Make sure the text on your slides is readable.

- Present the information in manageable sections.
- Lay it out clearly and consistently. The use of Slide Layouts helps in this respect since text placeholders are already formatted and slide titles, for example, are all in the same position. This makes it easy on the eye of the audience as one slide replaces another.
- Do not use very fancy fonts.
- Avoid too much emphasis and too many different methods of emphasis.
- Make sure the font size is large enough for your audience.
- Try not to include more than five or six points on one slide.
- Do not fill every available space on the slide. Leave space around the text to ensure the message can be seen.

Information: Formatting

To format text means to change its appearance. This includes choice of font, size, style, emphasis and alignment. The slide layouts you have used so far come with pre-determined formatting. Sometimes you will want to change this.

Font	Most fonts are either **serif** or **sans serif**. Serifs are little strokes at the ends of characters which sans serif characters do not have. **Times New Roman** is a serif font. **Arial** is sans serif. Serif is easier to read for normal text whilst sans serif is considered clearer for presentations. A huge number of fonts are available, e.g. **Comic Sans**, *Mistral*. They can be traditional, formal, fun, quirky, etc. Many are not suitable for presentations as they would be difficult to read. Choose carefully.
Font size	Size 44 is the usual default size for headings with 32 for body text size. Font sizes are measured in points – the higher the number, the larger the font, e.g. 16 point, 18 point, 20 point. Different fonts can appear to be different sizes even set at the same size.
CAPITALS	Capitals are used to make words stand out, especially headings.
Bold	The term 'to embolden text' means to make it bold, which is heavier and darker than normal text. Bold is frequently used to make words more noticeable, especially headings.
Italics	Italics are also used for emphasis, usually within the main body of text.
Underline	Underline is not used as much as bold, however it is sometimes useful for giving emphasis to particular words.
Shadow	This may be used for headings and emphasis, however it can sometimes make text look blurred.

Information

The **Formatting** toolbar holds the necessary buttons for fonts, size, emphasis and alignment.

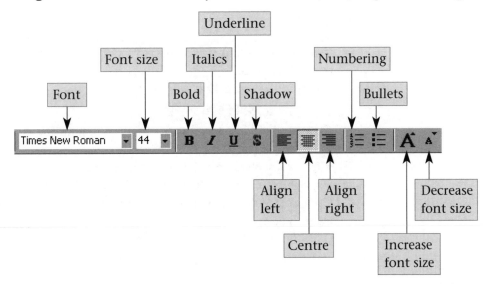

Figure 3.2 Formatting toolbar

- **To format text by changing font or font size**   Select existing text and click on the arrow alongside the font box to reveal a drop down list of fonts (Figure 3.3). For a choice of fonts, scroll through the font list by clicking on the up and down scroll buttons (Figure 3.4). Do the same for font size or click on **Increase** or **Decrease font size** button.

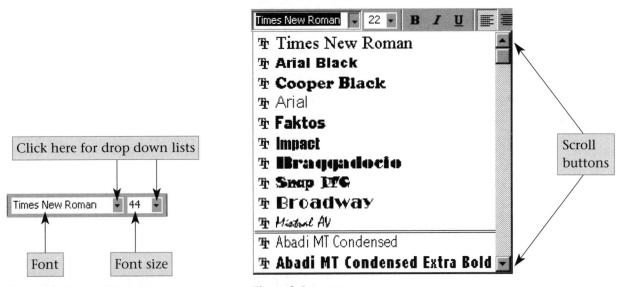

Figure 3.3 Fonts and font size

Figure 3.4 Font list

- **To format text by changing style of emphasis**   Select existing text and click on **Bold**, **Italics**, **Underline** or **Shadow** button as required (Figure 3.2). This is known as changing the font attributes.

These options can also be chosen prior to keying in new text.

Remember:

If you move the mouse over a toolbar button, a screen tip will appear.

Task 3.2 — Format and emphasise text

Method

1 Open the **Greenfingers** presentation if not already open and move to the first slide.
2 Highlight the word **Greenfingers**.
3 Click on the **Bold** button **B**
4 Click on the drop down arrow beside the font box and select **Arial** from the list (scroll down if necessary).
5 Click on **Increase font size** twice until size is 54.
6 Highlight the subtitle **Your Local Garden Centre**.
7 Click on the drop down arrow beside the font box and select **Arial** from the list.
8 With the subtitle still highlighted click on the Shadow button **S**
9 Move to the second slide and highlight the title **Stockists of**.
10 Change the font to **Arial**, make it bold and increase the size to 48.
11 Move to the third slide and highlight the title **Sundry Supplies**.
12 Change the font to **Arial**, make it bold and increase the size to 48.
13 Save the file.

Hint:

Formatting can be carried out in Outline or Slide pane.

Information: Text alignment

Align Left Text is aligned to the left of the text placeholder (Figure 3.5).
Centré Text is centred in the middle of the placeholder.
Align Right Each line ends at the right side of the placeholder.

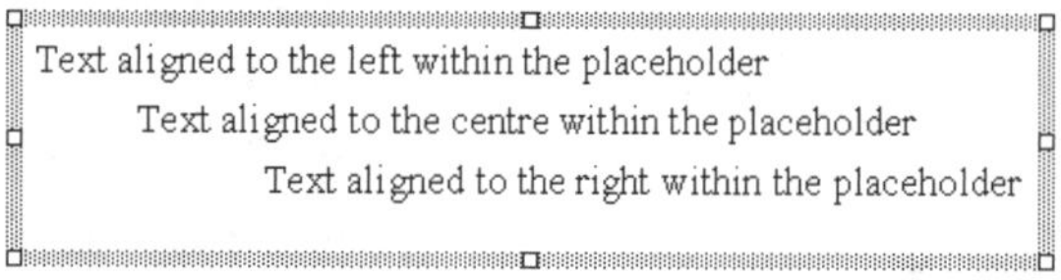

Text aligned to the left within the placeholder
Text aligned to the centre within the placeholder
Text aligned to the right within the placeholder

Figure 3.5 Alignment

Task 3.3 — Align text

Method

1 Using the same presentation, move to the second slide.
2 Position the cursor anywhere in the title.
3 Click on the **Align Left** button
4 Repeat on the third slide.
5 Do not save yet.

Information: Save As

So far you have used the Save button to save files. The first time a file is saved you must name it. When you subsequently save it by the same method, you are not prompted for a name as it already has one. Any changes you have made overwrite the original.

There may, however, be occasions when you wish to save a new version of a presentation with any amendments, but keep the original intact. This is when you use **Save As**, meaning you **Save** a presentation **As** something else, i.e. by another name. The new name can be similar or completely different, but of course should always reflect the content. It is often used to give systematic names to each version of a file, e.g. **Greenfingers version 2**, or simply **Greenfingers 2**. **Save As** can also be used for saving a presentation to another location.

Remember:

Always save a presentation with a name that will be recognisable later.

Task 3.4 — Save a presentation using a new name

You are going to save **Greenfingers** with a new name to preserve the original. Note the existing filename in the title bar at the top of the screen before you do this.

Method

1   Using the open file **Greenfingers** click on the **File** menu and select **Save As**.
2   Key in the filename **Greenfingers 2**.
3   Click on **Save**. Note the new filename in the title bar.

Remember:

Editing means to change the content, formatting means to change the appearance.

Task 3.5 — Add a footer

If you are sharing a printer with others it would be useful to add your name to the presentation as a footer before printing. A footer is text that appears at the bottom of every slide or page.

Method

1   Click on **View** menu and select **Header and Footer**.
2   Key in your name in the footer box.
3   Click on **Apply to All**.

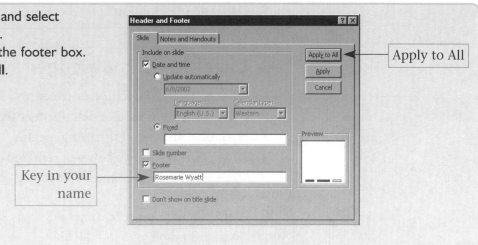

Key in your name

Apply to All

Figure 3.6 Add a footer

Task 3.6   Print a presentation

Note:

You will find out about print options later.

Method

Click on the **Print** icon

This causes the presentation to print one slide to a page.

→ Practise your skills 1

1 Open the presentation **Portway Homes**.
2 Change the font of the first slide to Verdana and make it bold.
3 Increase the size of the title to 54.
4 Increase the size of the subtitle to 40.
5 Change the title of the remaining two slides to Verdana, make them bold, apply a shadow effect and increase the size to 48.
6 Change these same two titles to left alignment.
7 Add your name as a footer.
8 Save as **Portway Homes 2**.
9 Print.
10 Close the presentation.

→ Practise your skills 2

1 Open the presentation **Health and Safety**.
2 Change the font of the title on the first slide to Arial, embolden, apply shadow effect and increase the size to 48.
3 Change the font of the subtitle to Arial, size 40 and bold.
4 Change the title of the second slide to Arial, apply bold and shadow effect and increase the size to 48.
5 Change the title to left alignment.
6 Add your name as a footer
7 Save as **Health and Safety 2**.
8 Print.
9 Close the presentation.

→ Check your knowledge

1 What is the quick method of selecting a single word?
2 What is the term used to describe text that is selected?
3 What does the term formatting mean?
4 What is the difference between serif and sans serif fonts?
5 Make a list of all the things you should consider when formatting text for a presentation.
6 When might you use Save As?
7 Give an example of a font attribute.

Consolidation 1

1 Open a new blank presentation and choose a title slide.

2 Key in the title **Dashwood House**.

3 Key in the subtitle **Family Hotel**.

4 Insert a new bulleted list slide and key in the title **Facilities**.

5 Key in the following as bullet points:

> **24 En-suite Bedrooms**
> **Bar and Restaurant**
> **Games Room**
> **Swimming Pool**
> **Residents Lounge**
> **Satellite TV**

6 Insert a new bulleted list slide and key in the title **Child-Friendly Facilities**.

7 Key in the following list as bulleted points:

> **Children's Playroom**
> **Video Library**
> **Baby Listening Service**
> **Family Rooms**
> **Laundry**

8 Spellcheck and proofread the presentation.

9 Add your name as a footer.

10 Save the presentation as **Dashwood House**.

11 Print.

12 Change the main title on the first slide to Helvetica (Arial if not available), bold with shadow effect.

13 Change the subtitle to Helvetica size 40.

14 Change the title on slides 2 and 3 to Helvetica, bold, size 40 and align left.

15 Change the bulleted lists on slides 2 and 3 to italics.

16 Save as **Dashwood House 2**.

17 Print.

18 Close the presentation.

Section 4

Working with graphical images

You will learn to

- Display the Drawing toolbar
- Insert clip art
- Resize and move clip art
- Search for clip art
- Insert graphics as files from various sources
- Use slide layout templates for clip art
- Change slide layouts

You can add interest to your presentations by illustrating them with graphical images. In this section you will incorporate clip art and find out how to use other images, such as photographs.

You should ideally have access to clip art and/or other graphic image files (e.g. photographic images) on disk or CD to carry out certain tasks, as well as access to the Internet.

Information: Using clip art

A variety of graphics can be used to illustrate presentations. One of these is clip art and PowerPoint has an in-built source of graphical images – the **clip gallery**.

Task 4.1   Display PowerPoint drawing toolbar

Method

1   Select **Toolbars** from the **View** menu. A side menu appears.
2   Click on **Drawing**.

The Drawing toolbar appears at the bottom of the window.

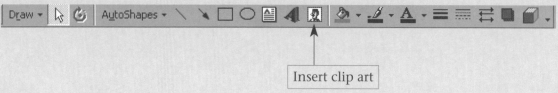

Insert clip art

Figure 4.1 Drawing toolbar

Task 4.2   Insert clip art, resize and move

Clip art is arranged in categories from which you select. It is also possible to search for an image using a keyword.

Method

1 Open a new presentation and select a title slide.
2 Key in the title **PowerPoint and Graphics**.
3 Key in your name as the subtitle.
4 Insert a new slide and choose the **Title Only** layout (Figure 4.2).

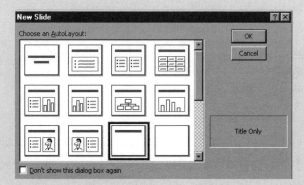

Figure 4.2 Title Only layout

5 Key in the title **Clip art from PowerPoint gallery**.
6 Click on **Insert Clip Art** button 🖼. Window appears (Figure 4.3).

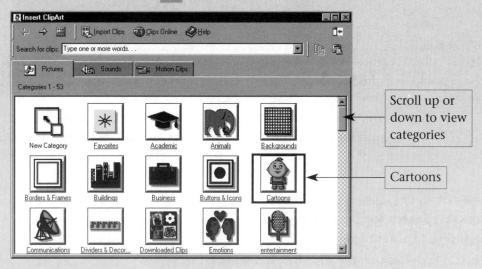

Figure 4.3 Clip art categories

7 Scroll down and click on a category, e.g. Cartoons.
8 View the images by scrolling down and click on any one to select it (Figure 4.4). Your images may be different to those shown.

Figure 4.4 Insert clip art

9	Click on **Insert clip** (Figure 4.4).
10	Close clip art window by clicking on ⊠. Image appears on the slide with 'handles' around the sides (Figure 4.5).
11	Position pointer over a corner handle (pointer changes to a diagonal double-headed arrow ↖) and drag inwards towards the middle of the image to make it smaller.
12	Position pointer over the image – it changes to a four-headed arrow ⊕. Hold down the mouse button and drag the image to a new position on the left.
13	Repeat from step 6 above to place a second image on the right.
14	Save the presentation as **Graphics**.

Figure 4.5 Resize image

Hint:

Always resize using a corner handle to keep the image in proportion.

Information

You can also move graphic images by selecting and pressing any of the four directional arrows on the keyboard.

Hint:

To delete a graphic image, click on it to select (handles appear) and press **Delete** on the keyboard.

Task 4.3	Search for clip art

You may frequently have to find clip art to match a specific topic that you are working on. To find what you want you will need to use the Search facility.

Method

1	Insert a new Title Only slide.
2	Key in the title **Search for clip art**.
3	Click on **Insert Clip Art** button 🖼
4	Key in **castle** in the **Search for clips** box and press **Enter**.

Search word →

Figure 4.6 Search for clip art

5	From the images displayed (yours may be different), select one and click **Insert clip** as before.
6	Close the ClipArt window.
7	Resize and reposition the image on the left.
8	Repeat from step 3 above to search for an image of a **horse**.
9	Resize and reposition the image on the right.
10	Save the presentation.

Clip art can also be obtained from floppy disk or from a CD, in which case the images would be inserted as files. Other graphical objects are inserted as files as well. These include:

- **Bitmap images** produced by a paint type program and usually characterised by a .bmp file extension.
- **Drawn graphics** produced and saved as **drawings**. Examples of file extensions are .drw, .cdr and .wmf.
- **Scanned images** produced by scanning pictures or drawings with a .bmp. .tif or .jpg file extension.
- **Digital photographic images** produced by a digital camera and often compressed (to make the file smaller and take up less storage space) and saved with a .jpg extension.

The last two are often saved in a compressed format (e.g. as .jpg) which means they are reduced in size and take up less storage space.

Task 4.4 — Insert graphics as files

If the graphic you require is stored on another drive or floppy disk or a CD, this is the procedure you should follow. You will need graphics stored on one of these storage mediums to try this.

Method

1. Insert a new Title Only slide.
2. Key in the title **Insert graphics as files**
3. If using a CD or floppy disk, insert into the appropriate drive (Figures 4.7 and 4.8).

Figure 4.7 CD drive

Figure 4.8 Floppy disk drive

For a CD, press the button below the drive and place CD onto the tray. Press the drive button for the tray to retract.

For a floppy disk, push the disk gently into the drive.

4 From the **Insert** menu, select **Picture**. A side menu appears (Figure 4.9).

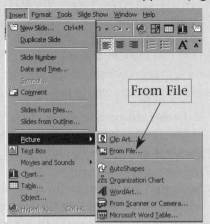

Figure 4.9 Insert picture

5 Select **From File**.
6 Click on down arrow alongside **Look in**: box (Figure 4.10).
7 Double click to select the required location. In this example **floppy disk drive A:** has been selected.

Figure 4.10 Select drive

8 Select image required and click on **Insert** (Figure 4.11).

Figure 4.11 Select graphic image

9 The graphic image appears on the slide. This image can be resized and moved in exactly the same way as clip art, either by selecting and dragging, or by selecting and using the arrow keys on the keyboard.

10	Add your name as a footer.
11	Save the presentation and print.
12	Close the presentation.

Hint:

You can also double click on a graphic image to select and insert it.

If you have access to more stored files, you should practise this process as you may be asked to do this in your end of module assignment.

Information: Graphic images from the Internet

Instructions for using the internet are beyond the scope of this book. If you have an Internet connection and are familiar with its use, PowerPoint's clip gallery has a direct link to it. On loading the clip gallery, click on Clips Online (Figure 4.12) and follow the links. Search for images by entering keywords in a similar way to Task 4.3 above. Right click on your chosen

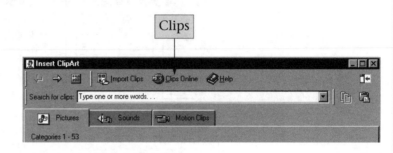

Figure 4.12 Clips from the Internet

image and either choose **Copy**, then paste the image into you presentation, or choose **Save Picture As**, and save to your work area. The image can then be inserted as a file into your presentation. These images can only be used for personal or non-commercial purposes.

A further source of clip art (and indeed photographic images) is the wider **Internet**. There are vast collections of these images available to choose from.
You must, however, check whether they are copyright-free before using them as they are often not free when used for commercial purposes.
Go to your usual search engine and search for **free clip art** or **free photos** (Figure 4.13). Navigate to one of the sites displayed and locate a suitable image. Copy or save it as above.

Figure 4.13 Search for clip art on the Internet

Hint:

Copyright means that the creator or owner has the right to control who can make copies and how their work can be used.

Hint:

When looking for images on the Internet, try different search engines for different results.

Remember:

Using slide layouts gives
consistency throughout a
presentation.

Task 4.5 — Using slide layouts to add clip art

Among the slide layouts available, there are layouts that aid the placing of
clip art. These help to ensure all clip art is in the same position on each
slide, as well as the text alongside it being consistent too.

Method

1   Open the presentation **Greenfingers 2**.
2   Move to the last slide and insert a new
    slide choosing **Text and Clip Art** (Figure 4.14).

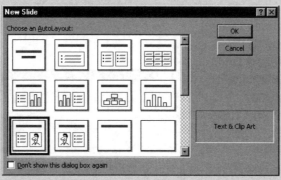

Figure 4.14 Text and clip art layout

3   Key in the title **Garden Ponds**. Change the font to Arial, size 48, bold and align left.
4   Add the following list as bullet points:

    Pond liners
    Fibreglass ponds
    Water plants
    Fish
    Pond design
    Pond construction

5   On the right-hand side of the slide, double click on the clip art icon to load the clip gallery. Search for
    a suitable image of **fish** and insert.
6   Save the presentation.

Task 4.6 — Change slide layouts

If you want to alter a slide layout, you can do this at any time.

Method

1   Move to slide 2 and click on **Common Tasks**
    on the Formatting toolbar.
    A menu drops down (Figure 4.15).

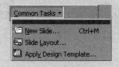

Figure 4.15 Common Tasks

2   Select **Slide Layout** and choose **Text and Clip Art**.
3   Double click on the **clip art** icon and search for a suitable **flower** image to insert.
4   Move to slide 3 and repeat this procedure searching for **garden tools**.
5   Save the presentation and print.

→ Practise your skills 1

1 Open the presentation **Portway Homes 2**.
2 Using the clip art button on the Drawing toolbar, insert an image to use as a logo on the first slide. (Search for **house** or **home**.)
3 Reduce the size of the image and move it above the title.
4 Move to slide 2 and change the layout to **Clip Art and Text**.
5 Insert a suitable image.
6 Repeat for slide 3.
7 Save the presentation and print.
8 Close the presentation.

→ Practise your skills 2

1 Open the presentation **Dashwood House 2**.
2 Using the clip art button on the Drawing toolbar, insert an image of the **sun** to use as a logo on the first slide.
3 Resize the image and position it above the title.
4 Move to slide 2 and change the layout to **Text and Clip Art**.
5 Insert a suitable image.
6 Move to slide 3.
7 If you have access to images on disk, CD or the Internet, insert a suitable image. If not, use clip art.
8 Save the presentation as **Dashwood House version 3** and print.
9 Close the presentation.

→ Check your knowledge

1 How can you resize an image?
2 How can you ensure an image is kept in proportion when resizing it?
3 What is a file extension?
4 How can you change a slide layout?
5 What action would you be performing when the pointer changes to this ✛?
6 What are the two methods of moving graphical objects?

Section 5

Running a slideshow and selecting print options

You will learn to

- Run a slideshow using the mouse
- Control a slideshow using the mouse
- Print selected slides
- Print handouts
- Print in black and white

In this section you will find out how to control a slideshow presentation and how to print slides in a variety of formats.

Information

For this module you are required to run a slideshow using a pointer device. The most common pointing device is, of course, the **mouse** which you are most likely to be using.

- **Mouse** This is moved across the desk to move the pointer, and one of the buttons (usually the left) is pressed to click. Some have a scroll wheel to aid moving around long documents, as in the example below (Figure 5.1).

Other devices are:

- **Touchpad** This is available on laptop computers. These are small, sensitive pads which you move your finger across to move the pointer and tap the pad to click, or there may be buttons to click (Figure 5.2).
- **Trackball** This is basically a mouse lying on its back. To move the pointer rotate the ball and tap the buttons either side of the ball to click (Figure 5.3).

Figure 5.1 Mouse

Figure 5.2 Touchpad

Figure 5.3 Trackball

If you are asked to deliver a presentation to an audience, e.g. at a meeting, you must be able to control how the slides appear.

Task 5.1 — Run a slideshow using the mouse

Method

1   Open the presentation **Dashwood House version 3**.
2   Click on **Slide Show** view (Figure 5.3). The presentation starts, the slide filling the screen.
3   To move to the next slide, click the left mouse button.
4   When you reach the end the screen turns black, click the mouse again to exit and return to Normal view.

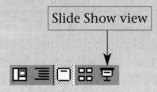

Slide Show view

Figure 5.4 Slide Show view

Task 5.2 — Control a slideshow using the mouse

When running a slideshow you may want to return to a previous slide or stop the show.

Method

1   Click on **Slide Show** view to start the slideshow.
2   Click the right mouse button – a menu appears.
3   Select **Next** to move to next slide.
4   Click the right mouse button and select **Previous**.
5   Click the right mouse button and select **End Show**.

Figure 5.5 Control a slideshow

Information: Printing presentations

So far you have printed one slide to a page using the print button, but there are further options. The **Print** dialogue box appears by selecting print from the **File** menu.

1 First select the **Print range** required – which slides you require to be printed.
2 Then select from **Print what:** choices – how you want them to be printed.

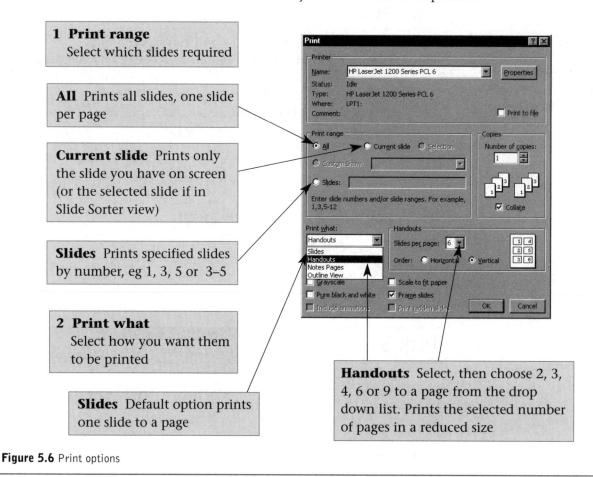

1 Print range
Select which slides required

All Prints all slides, one slide per page

Current slide Prints only the slide you have on screen (or the selected slide if in Slide Sorter view)

Slides Prints specified slides by number, eg 1, 3, 5 or 3–5

2 Print what
Select how you want them to be printed

Slides Default option prints one slide to a page

Handouts Select, then choose 2, 3, 4, 6 or 9 to a page from the drop down list. Prints the selected number of pages in a reduced size

Figure 5.6 Print options

Task 5.3   Choose Print options

Method

Print current slide
1   Using the same presentation, move to the first slide and select **Print** from the **File** menu.
2   Click on **Current slide**.
3   Click **OK**.

Print selected slides
4   Select **Print** from the **File** menu.
5   In the **Print range**, click on **Slides**.
6   In the **Print range** box, key in **2–3**.
7   Click **OK**.

Print handouts

8   Select **Print** from the **File** menu.
9   Select **All** for the Print range.
10 Select **Handouts** from the drop down **Print what:** list.
11 Click OK.

Print handouts 2 to a page

12 Select **Print** from the **File** menu.
13 Select **Handouts** from the drop down **Print what:** list.
14 Select **2** from drop down **Slides per page** menu.
15 Click **OK**.

Print handouts 3 to a page

16 Select **Print** from the **File** menu.
17 Select **Handouts** from the drop down **Print what:** list.
18 Select **3** from drop down **Slides per page** list.
19 Click **OK**.
20 Close the presentation.

The last three printouts should look like those in Figure 5.7.

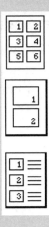

Figure 5.7 Handouts

Information: Printing in black and white

Whilst presentations for slideshows are produced for screen use, when printed out on a mono printer any colours will be printed in shades of grey. If you do not want this to happen, select **Pure Black and White** at the bottom of the Printer dialogue box to hide all shades of grey. Any objects with a fill colour will have no fill. This does not affect coloured clip art or photographic images which will still print with shades of grey.

→ Practise your skills 1

1 Open the presentation **Greenfingers 2**.
2 Run the slideshow using the mouse only.
3 Print as handouts 4 to a page.
4 Close.

→ Practise your skills 2

1 Open the presentation **Portway Homes 2**.
2 Run the slideshow using the mouse only.
3 Repeat, but when you reach the end, use the mouse to move back through the slideshow to the first slide.
4 Use the mouse only to stop the slideshow.
5 Print the first slide as a single slide.
6 Print the remaining slides as handouts 2 to a page.
7 Close.

→ Check your knowledge

1 What is the **Esc** key and what does it do?
2 Which button is used to start a slideshow? (Figure 5.8)

Figure 5.8

3 How can you print one slide only?
4 How does a handout printed 3 slides to a page differ from other printed handouts?

Consolidation 2

1 Open a new presentation and select a suitable slide for the title – **Pointer devices**.
2 Insert a suitable clip art graphic to illustrate and place below the title.
3 Insert a new slide titled **Mouse**.
4 List the following in bullet format:
    Move mouse across the desk to move pointer
    Press button to click and select
    Sometimes have a scroll wheel
    Most common device
5 Insert suitable clip art on the right.
6 Insert a new slide titled **Touchpad**.
7 List the following in bullet format:
    Available on laptop computers
    Small, sensitive pads
    Move finger across to move pointer
    Tap the pad to click and select
8 Insert a suitable clip art on the right.
9 Insert a new slide titled **Trackball**.
10 List the following in bullet format:
    A mouse lying on its back
    Rotate the ball to move the pointer
    Tap buttons either side of ball to click
11 Insert suitable clip art on the right.
12 Spellcheck and proofread.
13 Save the presentation with a suitable name.
14 Enlarge all the title fonts, change to Arial and embolden them.
15 Align the titles of slides 2, 3 and 4 to the left.
16 Change the layout of the slides with bullets and clip art so the clip art is on the left.
17 Add your name as a footer.
18 Save the presentation using the same suitable name and add **version 2**.
19 Run the slideshow through using the mouse.
20 Run through again, using the mouse to move backwards, forwards and to end the show.
21 Demonstrate this to your tutor.
22 Print the presentation as handouts 2 to a page.

If you have access to graphic images on CD or disk:	**If you have access to the Internet:**
1 Using the same presentation, delete the clip art and replace it with images inserted from disk or CD.	1 Using the same presentation, delete the images and replace with images found on the Internet.
2 Save it with the same name **version 3**.	2 Save with the same name **version 4**.
3 Print slides 2, 3 and 4 as handouts 3 to a page.	3 Print as handouts 4 to a page.
4 Print the first slide as a single slide.	4 Close the presentation.

Creating and modifying graphical objects

You will learn to

- Insert objects – lines and other shapes
- Move objects
- Modify objects
- Delete objects
- Rotate and flip objects
- Print in black and white

PowerPoint has a number of tools for drawing graphical objects such as lines and shapes. These can be used singly or combined together to create more complex objects such as diagrams.

Information: Inserting graphical objects

It is important to recognise that every text placeholder and image you have used so far is a separate object on a slide. In this section you will create graphical objects (lines and shapes) and manipulate them.

Ensure the drawing toolbar is displayed (**View** menu – **Toolbars** – **Drawing**).

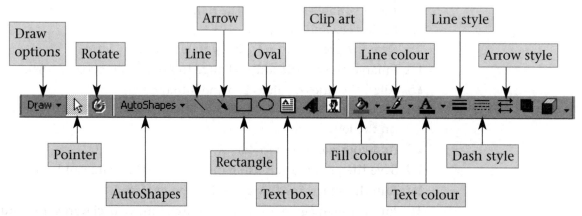

Figure 6.1 Drawing toolbar

Remember:

Move the mouse over a Toolbar button and a screen tip will appear.

Task 6.1 — Insert graphical objects – lines and other drawn shapes

Method

1. Start a new presentation with a blank slide.
2. Click on the **Line** button.
3. Position the crosshair where the line is to start.
4. Hold down the left mouse button and drag a few centimetres across the slide.
5. Release mouse.
6. Click on the **Arrow** button.
7. Draw in the same way – drag in the direction you require arrow to point to. Release mouse.
8. Click on the **Rectangle** button.
9. Position the crosshair where the rectangle is to start.
10. Drag a few centimetres across and down. Release mouse.
11. Click on the **Oval** button.
12. Draw in the same way – drag a few centimetres across and down. Release mouse.

Remember:

Drag the mouse means to hold down the left mouse button, move the mouse in the required direction and then release.

Remember:

Hold down the shift key when creating shapes for perfect lines, squares and circles.

Task 6.2 — Move objects

Note: When moving objects do not drag on a handle as this changes the size.

Method

1. Click on the **line** to select it (handles appear each end).
2. Hold down the left mouse button and drag on the line itself (not a handle) to move to new position.
3. Release mouse button.
4. Click on the **arrow** and move in the same way.
5. Click inside the **rectangle** to select.
6. Drag and move in the same way.
7. Click inside the **oval** and move in the same way.

Hint:

If an object shape has No Fill, drag on the edge to move.

Remember:

You can also move objects by selecting and using the arrow keys on the keyboard.

Task 6.3 — Change length or size of drawn objects

Once you have drawn an object you may want to change its length and size.

Method

1. Click on the **line** to select it.
2. Drag a handle to make it longer.
3. Click on the **arrow** and resize it in the same way.
4. Click on the **rectangle**.
5. Drag a handle inwards towards the middle to make it smaller, drag outwards to make it bigger.
6. Click on the **oval** and resize in the same way.

Hint:

When resizing a rectangle or an oval, hold down the shift key and drag a corner handle to keep it the same original shape.

Task 6.4 | Change the line style of any drawn object

Method

1 Select the **line**.
2 Click on **Line style** button (Figure 6.1) and choose a line weight (thickness) or style.
3 Click on **Dash style** and choose a style.
4 Select the **arrow** and click on the **Arrow style** button.
5 Choose a double-ended arrow style.
6 Change the line style for the other shapes.

Task 6.5 | Change fill

Method

1 Select the **rectangle**.
2 Click on the down arrow beside **Fill Color** button.
3 Choose from **No Fill** or one of the colours shown, or click on **More Fill Colors** (Figures 6.2 and 6.3).
4 Repeat for **oval** shape.

Figure 6.2 Fill color

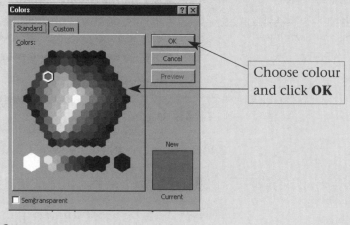

Figure 6.3 Colors

Hint:

When moving a shape with No Fill, you must drag on the edge of the shape.

Line colour can be changed in the same way by clicking on the down arrow by the **Line Color** tool. Try this too.

Task 6.6   Delete objects

Method

1. Select any object.
2. Press **Delete** key.
3. Repeat for all objects.

Task 6.7   Insert AutoShapes

Method

1. Click on the **AutoShapes** button on the Drawing toolbar – menu appears.
2. Click on **Stars and Banners** category.
3. Click on the **5-point Star**.
4. Position crosshair and drag mouse across and down.
5. Experiment with other categories of AutoShapes.

Hint:

Hold Shift key down to keep AutoShape in original proportion.

Figure 6.4 AutoShapes

Task 6.8   Insert freehand line

Method

1. Click on the **AutoShapes** button – select **Lines**.
2. Click on **Scribble**.
3. Hold down left mouse button and draw a wavy line.

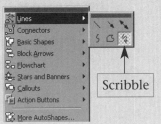

Hint:

Arrow styles can be applied to lines like this too.

Figure 6.5 Freehand lines

Task 6.9 — Rotate and flip objects

To **rotate** an object – moves it round in a circular direction.
To **flip horizontally** – displays its **mirror** image.
To **flip vertically** – turns it **upside down** or **inverts** it.

Method

1 Insert a new blank slide.
2 Select **Basic Shapes** from **AutoShapes**.
3 Click on the **Lightning Bolt** and draw the shape on the slide.
4 Click on the **Draw** button on the Drawing toolbar and select **Rotate or Flip**.
5 Click on **Rotate Left**.
6 Repeat selecting **Rotate Right**.
7 Repeat selecting **Flip Horizontal** and then **Flip Vertical**.

Task 6.10 — Rotate an object to any angle

Method

1 Click on the Lightning Bolt object drawn above to select.
2 Click on the **Free Rotate** button ⟳ on the Drawing toolbar. (The handles change to little circles.)
3 Drag one of the circular handles around in a circular movement in the direction you want to rotate the shape.

Try this with a text box. Create a text box and key in your name. Then rotate.

Information: Printing in black and white

You have already learnt that whilst presentations for slideshows are produced for screen use, when they are printed out on a mono printer any colours will be printed in shades of grey. If you do not want this to happen, select **Pure Black and White** at the bottom of the Print dialogue box to hide all shades of grey. Any objects with a fill colour will have no fill. This could be a problem if you have diagrams including shapes in colour, but does not affect coloured clip art or photographic images which will still print with shades of grey. Create a blank slide and insert filled shapes and coloured clip art and try this out.

Figure 6.6 Print in black and white

→ Practise your skills 1

1 Create a new presentation with a blank slide.
2 Reproduce the shapes shown in Figure 6.7 in roughly the same position.
3 Add your name as a footer, save as **Shapes** and print.

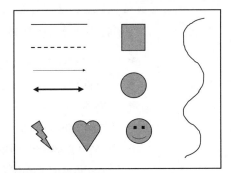

Figure 6.7 Graphical objects

→ Practise your skills 2

1 Using the slide from the previous task, change the colour of each of the **lines** so each one is a different colour.
2 Change the **double-headed arrow** to a different arrow style.
3 Change the **dashed line** to a different dash line style and make it longer.
4 Make the **solid line** shorter.
5 Make the **single arrow line** heavier (thicker).
6 Change the fill of the shapes so that each one is a different colour.
7 Flip the **lightning bolt** horizontally.
8 Flip the **heart** vertically.
9 Rotate the **smiley face** to the right.
10 Make the **circle** and the **rectangle** bigger.
11 Save as **Shapes version 2**. Print.
12 Move all the objects to a new position.
13 Save as **Shapes version 3**. Print.
14 Use **Free Rotate** tool to rotate each object.
15 Save as **Shapes version 4**. Print.
16 Close the presentation.

→ Check your knowledge

1 How do you turn an object into a mirror image of itself?
2 What is an inverted object?
3 How can you draw a perfect circle?
4 What must you not drag on when moving an object?
5 If a shape object has No fill, how can you move it?

Section 7

Manipulating graphical objects

You will learn to

- Copy and paste objects
- Layer objects
- Order layers
- Group objects
- Resize grouped objects
- Create and modify a text box
- Group text with other objects
- Position objects using the ruler

Information: Copy and paste

Copying an object allows you to place the copy elsewhere in a presentation, another presentation or even another application, whilst keeping the original in place. When you **copy** an object, the copy is held in an area of memory called the **clipboard** ready to **paste** into the document. You can also **cut** objects from their current position to remove them altogether and paste them into a new position. These features also work with text, clip art and other objects.

Task 7.1   Copy and paste objects

Method

1   Start a new presentation and a blank slide.
2   Draw a small rectangular box shape.
3   Click on the rectangle to select (if not already selected).
4   Click on the **Copy** button on the Standard toolbar (Figure 7.1).

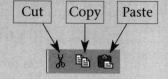

Figure 7.1 Copy and paste

5   Click on **Paste**. A copy appears on top of the original.
6   Move the copy and change the fill colour.
7   Click on **Paste** again and a further copy appears.
8   Move the copy and change the fill colour.

Task 7.2 — Copy and paste to another slide

Method

1. Select one of the shapes drawn above.
2. Click on **Copy**.
3. Insert a new blank slide.
4. Click on **Paste**.
5. Return to the first slide and repeat for the remaining two shapes.

Information: Layer and order objects

Sometimes you might need to position one object on top of another, or add some text on top of an object. When objects overlap, you can decide in which order they should be layered. This is called **ordering**. Imagine several sheets of paper in a pile, one on top of the other, you can decide which to send to the back of the pile, which to bring to the front and so on.

Task 7.3 — Layer and order objects

Method

1. Position the three boxes so that they overlap as in Figure 7.2.

Figure 7.2 Overlapping shapes

2. Select the box at the front 'on the top of the pile'.
3. Click on the **Draw** button on the Drawing toolbar and select **Order**. A side menu appears (Figure 7.3).

Figure 7.3 Order objects

4   Select **Send to back**.

5   Select the middle layer, click on **Draw** button, select **Order** then **Bring to Front**.

6   With the same layer selected, click on **Draw** button, select **Order** then **Send Backward**.

Information: Group objects

When working with several objects, it is sometimes easier to group them together, for repositioning, copying and resizing.

Task 7.4   Group and ungroup objects

Method 1

1   Position pointer at point 1 in Figure 7.4 and drag across and down to point 2. When mouse button is released, handles appear on all objects enclosed in that space.

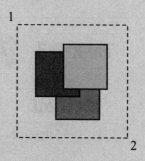

Figure 7.4 Select Group and Ungroup objects

2   Click on the **Draw** button and select **Group**.

3   Drag the group to a new position.

4   Whilst selected, click on **Draw** button and choose **Ungroup**.

5   Click on a blank area of the screen to deselect.

Method 2

1   Hold down the **Shift** key and click in turn on each of the boxes.

2   Click on the **Draw** button and select **Group**.

Task 7.5   Copy and resize grouped object

Method

1   Select the grouped object and click on **Copy** button

2   Click **Paste** button

3   Move the copy to a new position.
4   Select one of the grouped objects.
5   Reduce the size by dragging a corner handle towards the middle of the object.
6   Enlarge by dragging outwards.
7   Close the presentation – you do not need to save.

Information: Text box objects

The text boxes you have used so far have been part of a slide's layout, in the form of placeholders. You can create your own text boxes of any shape and size, to hold titles, normal text, bulleted lists and small text labels as well. If the text box is not wide enough for the text and wraps onto a second line, resize it to make it wider. Text boxes you create do not show in the Outline window.

Task 7.6   Create a text box

Method

1   Open a new presentation.
2   Insert a new blank slide.
3   Click on the **Text Box** tool 📧 on the Drawing toolbar.
4   Position the crosshair towards the top of the slide and press and drag across about halfway and release. The cursor will flash inside the text box.
5   Key in **Manipulating objects**.
6   Click on the **Text Box** tool and draw a smaller text box.
7   Key in **PowerPoint**.

Task 7.7   Resize and move a text box

Method

1   Click on one of the text boxes created above to select if not already selected.
2   Drag a side handle of the text box to make it wider.
3   Drag a side handle to make it smaller so that it is just big enough for the text.
4   Repeat for the second text box.
5   Click on the edge of one of the text boxes to select – the shading of the line changes slightly if you watch closely.
6   Press and drag on the edge of the text box to move it. (Do not drag a handle or you will resize the text box.)

Task 7.8 | Group text with other objects

Method

Remember:

Save your presentation regularly as you work.

1 Using the same slide as above, click on the **Rectangle** tool and draw a shape bigger than the PowerPoint text box.
2 Select a **Star** shape from the **Stars and Banners** category of **AutoShapes** and draw a star.
3 Change the fill colour of the star.
4 Move it on top of the rectangle.
5 Move the PowerPoint text box on top of the star. (It may disappear behind the other shapes.)
6 Order the layers to appear as Figure 7.5.

Figure 7.5 Grouped objects

7 Select all three objects using one of the methods used in Task 7.4 above.
8 Click on **Draw** button and select **Group**.
9 Save as **Working with objects**.

Information: More about grouped objects

- Whilst you can resize objects grouped with text, the text does not resize and may need adjusting separately.
- You can still edit text when grouped with other objects (if the text box is big enough).
- When selecting or moving objects grouped with text, do not click on the text to drag as this puts you into text edit mode.
- If you **Ungroup** several objects and adjust them, you can click on any one and click on **Draw – Regroup**, to group them together again without reselecting.

Remember:

It is much easier to move grouped objects than to move them separately.

Information: Align text and graphical objects

You may sometimes wish to line up text and objects accurately; to do this you use the rulers. If the ruler at the top and left side of the slide window is not displayed, select **Ruler** from the **View** menu. Using Slide view, move the mouse across the slide without clicking. As you do so, you should see a vertical marker line in the ruler moving with the mouse indicating the current position. If you move the mouse up and down and look at the ruler on the left of the slide window, you will see a corresponding horizontal marker line moving. The ruler changes its appearance depending on what object you select. If you select an image or shape, the ruler's origin (the start point) is in the middle. If you select the edge of a text box, its origin is at the left. If you select text inside a text box, the ruler changes again.

Task 7.9	Align text and graphical objects using the ruler

1 Align vertically
Method

1. Use the open presentation **Working with objects**.
2. Create a text box below the grouped objects and key in **Grouped objects**. Resize the text box to fit the text.
3. Select the text box **Manipulating graphics** and drag on its edge until the marker in the top ruler reads **2** to the left of the middle of the slide (Figure 7.6).

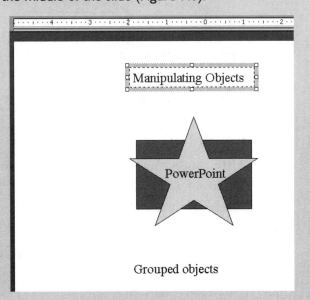

Figure 7.6 Using the top ruler

4. Select the grouped objects and position them below the text at the same point.
5. Repeat for the second text box.

2 Align horizontally
Method

1   Move the first text box so that it aligns with the marker in the side ruler at **1** on the scale (Figure 7.7).
2   Repeat for the grouped objects.

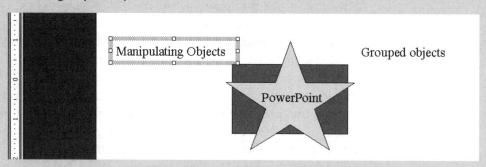

Figure 7.7 Using the side ruler

3   Repeat for the second text box if you have the space.
4   Save and close.

→ Practise your skills 1

1   Open a new presentation with a blank slide.
2   Select the AutoShape **Chevron** from the Block Arrows category and draw the shape (Figure 7.8).

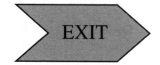

Figure 7.8 Exit sign

3   Copy and paste the shape.
4   Flip one of the shapes horizontally.
5   Select the **Text box** tool and draw a text box.
6   Key in the text **EXIT**.
7   Move the text onto one of the chevrons.
8   Create another text box and key in the words **WAY IN**.
9   Move the text onto the other chevron.
10 Group each of the chevrons with their text label.
11 Create a text box and key in **SIGNS**.
12 Line up the text box and the two grouped objects down the page using the ruler.
13 Insert a new blank slide.
14 Copy the Exit sign from slide 1 and paste onto the new slide.
15 Save as **Signs**.
16 Print slides as a handout 2 to a page.
17 Close.

→ Practise your skills 2

1 Open a new presentation and a blank slide.

2 Reproduce the picture in Figure 7.9 using boxes, circles and a text box, different fill colours, and ordering techniques to put layers into a suitable order.

Figure 7.9 Lorry

3 Group the objects together.

4 Copy the grouped object and paste it twice.

5 Make one copy smaller than the original, ensuring that the original proportion is maintained.

6 Adjust the size of the text as necessary.

7 Make the other copy larger than the original, maintaining the proportions.

8 Adjust the text size as necessary.

9 Insert a new slide and copy and paste the smallest version onto it.

10 Flip the picture horizontally.

11 Create a text box and key in the text **Our new fleet!**

12 Line up the picture with the text box across the page.

13 On the first slide, **Ungroup** the largest image and rotate the text box so that it runs diagonally across the side of the lorry. Regroup it.

14 Save the presentation as **County Removals**.

15 Print as a handout 2 to a page.

16 Close.

→ Check your knowledge

1 What is the clipboard?

2 If you have drawn 3 overlapping shapes and send the 'top' one **Backward**, what does this mean?

3 Apart from dragging around a group of objects to select them all, what is the other method you can use?

4 How do you move a text box?

5 If you **Ungroup** several objects to adjust them, what is the quick way of grouping them together again?

Consolidation 3

If possible locate two holiday photographic images on CD or disk, or find two images from the Internet and save to your work area.

1 Open a new presentation and choose a title slide.
2 Key in the title **COMPASS HOLIDAYS**.
3 Key in the subtitle **Faraway destinations**.
4 Above the title, create the compass logo as in Figure 7.10. Use the AutoShape **4-point star** and a separate text box for each of the points.

Figure 7.10 Compass

5 Line up the W and E text boxes horizontally, and the N and S ones vertically.
6 Group the compass objects together.
7 Position the compass so that the North point is below the **0** on the top ruler.
8 Insert a new Bulleted list slide.
9 Key in the title **WHAT WE OFFER**.
10 Key in the bulleted list as follows:

Escorted tours
Experienced Guides
Tried and tested destinations
Recommended Hotels

11 Insert two photographic images and place to the right of the list, reducing in size but keeping them in proportion.
12 Line them up one beneath the other using the ruler.
13 Insert a new **Bulleted list** slide and key in the title **FEATURES OF OUR TOURS**.

Transport from your front door
Constant tour guide supervision
Two guides for each tour
No surcharge for singles
Group bookings a speciality

14 Copy and paste the logo from slide 1 and paste to the side of the list on slide 3.
15 Use Free Rotate to rotate the bottom of the logo towards the middle of the slide.
16 Insert a new **Text and Clip Art** slide
17 Key in the title **CURRENT DESTINATIONS**.

18 Key in the list:

India
Australia
South Africa
China

19 Insert a suitable image.
20 Spellcheck and proofread.
21 Save the presentation as **Compass Holidays**.
22 Run the slideshow using the mouse.
23 Print the slideshow as handouts 4 to a page.
24 Change the titles of each slide to Arial.
25 Change the layout of slide 4 to **Clip Art and Text**.
26 Save as **Compass Holidays 2**.
27 Print slide 4 only as one slide to a page.
28 Close the presentation.

You will learn to

- Import selected text from another application
- Set indents
- Set tabs
- Change page layout

For this section you will need basic knowledge of and access to a word processor, e.g. Word.

Information: Importing selected text

When creating a presentation you may sometimes have text already prepared by word processing or in a desktop publishing file, that you wish to use in a presentation. To save re-entering the text, it can be copied and pasted into the presentation.

Before starting this task, enter the following text into Word and save the file as **Compass**.

> We have visited all destinations many, many times and have established local contacts to ensure we have access to the very best local information.
>
> Our guides have many years travel experience between them and much local knowledge to give you the very best taste of the region you have chosen to travel to.
>
> If you have a group of people you want to travel with, then we are happy to arrange your trip. Equally you can join a group of like-minded people who will become good friends.

Task 8.1 Import selected text

Method

1 Start with all files and programs closed.
2 Load Word and open the word processed file **Compass**.
3 Highlight the text and click on Copy.
4 Load PowerPoint and open the presentation **Compass Holidays 2**.
5 Look at the taskbar at the bottom of the screen (Figure 8.1). This shows the two programs and files that are open. The name of the current file (the one visible onscreen) appears to be 'pressed in'. Click on each in turn to see how this works. End up with PowerPoint onscreen.

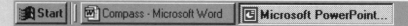

Figure 8.1 Taskbar

Remember:

You can always close a presentation without saving it if you want to revert to your previous version.

6　Move to the last slide and insert a new blank slide.
7　Select the **Text Box** tool and draw a text box across the top of the slide.
8　With the cursor flashing inside the text box, click on the **Paste** button.
9　Adjust the size of the text box or the size of text if necessary.
10　Save the presentation as **Compass Holidays 3**.

Information: Indenting text and bullets

Text is sometimes indented (moved to the right) to make it stand out from other text. Bullets are sometimes indented to make sub-bullets of the main points, e.g.

- Main bullet point
  - Sub-bullet
  - Sub-bullet
- Main bullet point

The easiest method of doing this is by using the **Demote** ➡ and **Promote** ⬅ buttons. If these do not appear on your Formatting toolbar, you must add them. **Demote** indents text and bullets to the right, and **Promote** moves them to the left.

Task 8.2　Add Promote and Demote buttons

Method

1　Click on **More buttons** at the end of the Formatting toolbar (not the Standard toolbar).
2　Click on **Add or Remove Buttons** (Figure 8.2).
3　Select **Promote** from the drop down menu.
4　Select **Demote**.
5　Click off the menu.

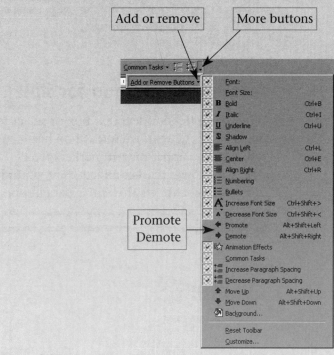

Figure 8.2 Add buttons

Task 8.3 — Indent text

Method 1

1. Use the slide created in the last task.
2. Click into the second paragraph.
3. Click on the **Demote** button ➡
4. Repeat for the third paragraph.
5. **Promote** ⬅ the second paragraph back to its previous position.
6. Repeat for the third paragraph.
7. Save the presentation.

Task 8.4 — Indent bullets

Method 1

1. Insert a new bulleted list slide and key in the title **TOUR GUIDES**.
2. Change the font to Arial
3. Key in the list:

   India
   John Kempson
   Marcella Martinez
   China
   Haizhu Lee
   David Wells

4. Click on **John Kempson** and click on **Demote** button.
5. Repeat for Marcella Martinez, Haizhu Lee and David Wells.
6. Save the presentation.

Alternative method for indenting

When you click inside a text box or select text, the ruler displays the indent markers for the text. Each text box has its own ruler and its own indent settings. The upper indent marker affects the first line of all paragraphs, whilst the lower marker affects the remainder. Dragging the rectangular part of this marker affects the entire paragraph.

Indent markers

Figure 8.3 Text ruler

Task 8.5   Indent text

Method 2

1. Move to the last slide and click in the first paragraph.
2. Drag the rectangular indent marker (Figure 8.3) to **1** on the ruler. Notice how all paragraphs move.
3. Drag it back again.

Task 8.6   Indent bullets

Method 2

The main bullets and sub-bullets have their own indent markers (Figure 8.4). The top marker indicates the bullet itself and the bottom marker the text.

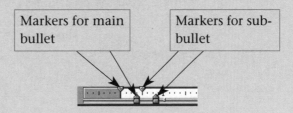

Markers for main bullet

Markers for sub-bullet

Figure 8.4 Bullet indent markers

1. Move to slide 6 – the list of tour guides.
2. Click on **John Kempson** and drag the rectangular indent marker *for the sub-bullet* to the right. Notice how all sub-bullets move.
3. Drag the marker back again.

Experiment with these markers and then close the presentation *without saving*.

Information: Using tabs

Tabulation is the arrangement of text and numbers in columns. This can be achieved by using **Tabs** which can be set across a slide at points where you wish to line up data.

By default, tabs are set every 1.27 cm ($\frac{1}{2}$ inch) across the slide. When a new tab is set, the default tabs to the left of it are cleared.

Task 8.7 — Use tabs

Method

1 Open the presentation **Compass Holidays 3**.
2 Insert a new Title Only slide at the end.
3 Key in the title **NEXT DEPARTURES**.
4 Change the font to Arial.
5 Draw a text box across the slide below the heading and key in **India**.
6 With the cursor still inside the text box, to set a tab click on the bottom of the ruler at **5** on the scale. A tab marker appears.
7 Press the **Tab** key on the keyboard and key in **March**.
8 Press **Enter** and key in **China**.
9 Press **Tab** key and key in **April**.
10 Press **Enter** and key in **South Africa**.
11 Press **Tab** key and key in **June**.
12 Press **Enter** and key in **Australia**.
13 Press **Tab** key and key in **September**.
14 Save the presentation.

Tab key

Figure 8.5 Tab key

Information: Page setup

As a presentation is usually created to run on a computer screen, the slides are set up by default, in landscape format – longer edge at the top. This orientation can be changed to portrait via the **File** menu and **Page Setup**. If this is done after creating a presentation, it can have an undesired effect on the placement of text and images.

Landscape

Portrait

PowerPoint does not have page margins like a word processing program. Text and objects can be placed right up to the edge of a slide, though a space around the edge is more pleasing to look at.

→ Practise your skills 1

1 Start a new presentation and select a **Title Only** slide.
2 Key in **Tour Guide Experience**.
3 Change the font to Arial.
4 Open Word and the word processed file **Compass**.
5 Copy the second paragraph.
6 Switch back to PowerPoint.
7 Draw a text box across the slide below the heading.
8 Paste in the copied text.
9 Draw another text box across the slide below the first one.
10 Key in **Guide** and embolden.
11 Click on the bottom edge of the ruler at **5** on the scale.
12 Press the **Tab** key, key in **Experience** and embolden.
13 Press **Enter** and key in **John Kempson**.
14 Press the **Tab** key and key in **10 years**.
15 Press **Enter**.
16 Complete the table as follows:

   Marcella Martinez   15 years
   Haizhu Lee   12 years
   David Wells   15 years

17 Align the main title to the left.
18 Line up the two text boxes you created with the text box tool, using the top ruler.
19 Insert your name as a footer.
20 Spellcheck and proofread.
21 Saves as **Guides**.

→ Practise your skills 2

1 Using the same presentation, insert a new Text and Clip Art slide
2 Key in the heading **Languages spoken**.
3 Start the list by keying in **Haizhu Lee** and press **Enter**.
4 Click on the **Demote** button to indent for a sub-bullet and key in **Mandarin**.
5 Press **Enter** and key in **Cantonese**.
6 Press **Enter** and click on **Promote** to return to a main bullet.
7 Key in **John Kempson** and press **Enter**.
8 Click on the **Demote** button to indent for a sub-bullet and key in **Hindi**.
9 Press **Enter** and key in **Panjabi**.
10 Insert suitable clip art on the right-hand side.
11 Save the presentation.
12 Print as a handout 2 slides to a page.

→ Check your knowledge

1 What are the purposes of indents?
2 How can you import selected text from another application into a presentation?
3 What is the purpose of tabs?
4 Which orientation is the default for slide presentation?
5 How do you set a tab marker?

Organising slides

You will learn to

- View and reorder slides
- Duplicate slides
- Delete slides

Information: Organising slides

The Slide Sorter view gives you an overview of all your slides in miniature to give you an idea of the finished look of your presentation. It enables you to change the order of the slides very easily by clicking on a slide and dragging to a new position. Slides can also be deleted in this view or duplicated by copying. You might want to copy a title slide to the end of a presentation to reinforce the title or to use an existing slide as the basis for a new one.

Task 9.1 — View and change the order of slides

Method

1. Open the presentation **Greenfingers**.
2. Click on **Slide Sorter** view button  in the bottom left of window (Figure 9.1). All slides appear.

Figure 9.1 Slide Sorter view

3. The selected slide has a dark blue border around it (Figure 9.2).

Figure 9.2 Slides in Slide Sorter view

4. Click on slide 2 – the slide is selected.
5. Click between the slides – a vertical line appears.
6. Click on the last slide and drag it between the first two slides.
   Note: The slide does not move until you release the mouse button.
7. Move the first slide to the end.
8. Move the same slide back to its previous position as the first slide.

Task 9.2 Duplicate a slide

Method

1   Click on the first slide – the title slide.
2   Click on the **Copy** 📑 button.
3   Click directly after the last slide.
4   Click on the **Paste** 📋 button.

Task 9.3 Delete slides

Method

1   Click on the last slide (the new one you pasted in).
2   Press **Delete** on the keyboard.

To move back to Slide view, either click on **Slide view** button or double click on one of the slides.

3   Close the presentation without saving.

Remember:

Click **Undo** if you make a mistake.

Information

Slides can also be moved, copied and deleted in the Outline pane by clicking on the required slide icon (Figure 9.3).

3 ▢ **Stockists of**
     • Bedding Plants
     • Perennials

Figure 9.3 Slide icon in Outline pane

→ Practise your skills 1

1   Open the presentation **Compass Holidays 3**.
2   Delete slide 6 (the slide titled Tour Guides).
3   Move the slide titled **Features of our Tours** to become slide 2.
4   Move the slide **Current Destinations** to become slide 3.
5   Move the slide titled **Next Departures** to become slide 4.
6   Copy the first slide (the title slide) to the end of the presentation.
7   Delete the slide with the three paragraphs of text.
8   Save as **Compass Final Version**.
9   Print as a handout 6 to a page.

→ Check your knowledge

1 How do you delete a slide?

2 How do you copy a slide?

3 How can you move a slide?

4 Why might you want to copy a slide?

Hardware requirements

You will learn to

- Identify the hardware requirements for graphics presentation software
- Identify the hardware requirements for presenting a slideshow

Information

Technology is changing all the time and computer equipment or hardware can become out of date very rapidly. Any figures given below are typical at the time of writing. For this reason, if you have a choice to make about hardware you should always choose the highest specification that you can. For up-to-date information, look at computer suppliers' web sites on the Internet.

Graphics presentation software

Graphics programs generally need more processing power and memory than for straightforward text processing. As you move graphical objects around, the computer needs to be able to handle them. Currently, a high specification computer might have the following:

Processor speed   2 GHz (Gigahertz)
Memory   256 Mb (Megabytes)

Presenting a slideshow

The following are the hardware you need for presenting a slideshow.

Display types

A standard 17-inch **computer monitor** might typically have a resolution of 1024 x 768, which means it can display 1024 dots (or pixels) on each of 768 lines, a total of around 790,000 pixels. The larger the monitor and the higher the resolution, the better.

A slideshow presentation is quite likely to be made to a group of people, for example at a meeting. Therefore a normal computer screen will not be large enough. You could use a **large screen monitor**. This might be a large television screen on a raised trolley to which a computer is connected.

Figure 10.1 Projector

Figure 10.2 Laptop computer

Another solution is to use a **projector** (Figure 10.1). This can be connected to an ordinary computer and the image is displayed on a projector screen. Projectors are also used in conjunction with **laptop computers** (Figure 10.2). This makes it quite easy for someone to travel to a venue to give a presentation, carrying a laptop computer loaded with presentation graphics software and a projector.

Portable storage

All the presentations you have created have been stored on a work area on your own computer or on a network. If you need to transport the presentation file itself to another location, you should consider the options for doing this. Each of the types of storage media below require relevant hardware. Clearly, if you are taking the file elsewhere you need to be sure that the necessary equipment is available for you to access. For example, most computers do not have zip drives. For up-to-date prices for each type, look at computer suppliers on the Internet.

Type of storage	Capacity	Features
Floppy disk	1.4 Mb	Requires the use of a floppy disk drive which is typically available on any desktop or laptop computer. Disks are very cheap to purchase. Storage capacity is not large.
Zip disk	100 Mb or 250 Mb	Requires a zip drive. A 100 Mb disk will work in a 100 or 250 Mb zip disk drive, a 250 Mb disk in a 250 Mb drive only. Zip drives not typically available on most computers. Disks are expensive. Large storage capacity.
CD-R CD-W	650 Mb	Requires a CD-ROM drive or a CD Writer. CD-R can be recorded on once. CD-W can be recorded on more than once. Drives widely available on up-to-date computers. Disks are cheap. Very large storage capacity.
DVD-R DVD-W	4.7 Gb	Require a DVD recording device or player. Not as many computers have DVD drives as CD drives. Disks are quite expensive. Have huge storage capacity.

Figure 10.3 Storage

Printers

The most common types of printer are the **inkjet printer** and the **laser printer**.

- **Inkjet printers** work by using ink cartridges and spraying fine jets of ink onto the paper. The print quality can be good depending on the resolution of the printer. Resolution is measured in dpi (dots per inch) and the higher the resolution, the better the quality of the printout. An inkjet printer resolution might be around 720 dpi, which means it can print 720 distinct dots in a line one-inch long. These printers may be black and white only (mono), in which case they would have one ink cartridge, or if they are colour they will probably have 3 colour ink cartridges (separate or 3-in-1) and a black one. Typically, these printers can be slow and are not usually found in workplaces where a lot of printing is carried out.
- **Laser printers** are widely used in business and produce high quality printouts. They work using the same technology as photocopiers and use toner cartridges, which are expensive. Most lasers are black and white (mono) printers. Colour laser printers cost many hundreds of pounds. Resolution would typically be in the region of 1200 dpi.

If choosing a printer for graphics work, and cost is no object, choose the highest resolution colour laser with a fast output (i.e. number of pages printed per minute).

When working with graphics, colour is frequently used. Therefore if printouts are required, a high quality colour printer would be the favoured option. Printed colour does not always match what you see onscreen however, which can be a problem. If you are giving a presentation with PowerPoint, you may want to give your audience handouts. Black and white can be quite satisfactory for this purpose as colour will appear in shades of grey, but if you include colour-coded drawings or diagrams, then this will not show up clearly, if at all. If you do not want shades of grey, you can print in pure black and white (see Section 6 for printer options), in which case any PowerPoint objects filled with colour will appear to have none.

Pointer devices

Pointer devices are covered in Section 5.

→ Practise your skills 1

Create a presentation entitled Hardware using a different slide for each item, including:

- Computer
- Monitor
- Storage media
- Printers

If you have Internet access, search the Internet for computer suppliers to find information, current prices, and images as well.

→ Check your knowledge

1 What processor speed might you look for in a computer for graphics work?

2 What memory would you look for?

3 What size computer monitor would be best?

4 If you had to present a slideshow at a venue without a computer, what would you need to take with you?

5 Which of the *two* following types of storage media drives are available on most up-to-date computers?

Floppy disk
Zip disk
CD
DVD

6 Which is the better quality printer – an inkjet or a laser?

7 What are the problems of printing coloured slides on a mono printer?

Practice assignments

Practice assignment 1

Read the scenario before you start.

Scenario

You are employed by the head office of a manufacturing company and have been asked by the Training Officer, Gina Hughes, to put together a presentation on health and safety that she is to present to some managers on a Health and Safety course.

Slide 1
Health and Safety
Working with Computers

Slide 2
Office Chairs
(Picture on the right)
Adjustable height
Adjustable backs
Swivel seats
Wheels

Slide 3
Computer Screens
(Picture on the left)
Tiltable screens
Flicker-free
Non-reflective
Position to avoid glare from windows

Slide 4
Eye Strain
This can be a problem and staff should be encouraged to rest their eyes frequently and focus away from the screen from time to time. We can provide screen filters if requested. Please ensure that blinds are in use at all windows.
(Picture below text)

Slide 5
Repetitive Strain Injury
(Image below)
This is otherwise known as RSI and is caused by frequent wrist movement and poor posture. We provide wrist rests and staff must be encouraged to use them. Please ensure staff are aware of the dangers of RSI.

Slide 6
Reporting procedure
Diagram

Note: Use the filename Health and Safety.

Task A

Suitable text sizes should be used throughout.

1 Start the presentation package with a new file.

2 Use a suitable template (layout) for the first slide using suitable fonts and sizes.

3 Create slide 2 with a heading and a bulleted list with a suitable picture on the right.

4 Create slide 3 with a heading and a bulleted list with a picture on the left.

5 Create slide 4 with a heading. The text should spread across the slide with a suitable image below. Copy the image, reduce it to a small size and place it in the top right corner. Copy and paste it into the left corner. Line up the two images using the ruler.

6 Create slide 5 with a heading. An image should be placed below the heading. Text should spread across the slide.

7 Create slide 6 with a heading and diagram below it.
Draw a box and copy it twice. Make each a different colour. Add a text box to each with a white background.

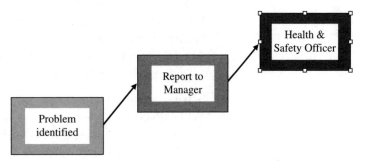

8 Spellcheck and proofread.

9 Add your name as a footer.

10 Save the slideshow presentation using the name specified above.

11 Print as a handout 6 to a page.

12 Change the boxes on slide 6 so they are all the same colour.

13 Move slide 6 (Reporting Procedures) so it becomes slide 2.

14 On the Computer Screens slide, indent the last bulleted item.

15 Save the new version of the slideshow with a new name, keeping the original.

16 Print again as a handout 6 slides to a page.

17 Print slide 5 as a single slide.

Task B

1 Demonstrate the slideshow to your tutor, controlling it with the mouse.

2 Close down the presentation and the presentation package. Hand in all printouts.

Practice assignment 2

You will need a photographic image of a man for this task. If you do not have access to one now, use the clip art gallery, but be aware that you may have to perform this task in the actual assignment and should therefore be familiar with what is required.

Read the scenario before you start.

Scenario

You are working as an administrator at Castle Hotel and Conference Centre. The manager has asked you to prepare a presentation that he is giving to a local trade organisation to promote the centre.

Slide 1
CASTLE HOTEL AND CONFERENCE CENTRE
Conferences and Weddings
(Logo at the bottom)

Slide 2
CONFERENCES
(List on the left, image on the right)
Fully serviced conferences for 50 up to 200
Gourmet catering
Special overnight accommodation rates
Regular customer discounts

Slide 3
WEDDINGS
Weddings luncheons, buffets and dinners
Cordon Bleu cuisine
Flowers
Music
Special overnight rates for guests
(Picture in bottom right)

Slide 4
CATERING SERVICES
(List on the right, image on the left)
Silver Service
Hot or cold buffet
Finger buffet
Refreshments

Slide 5
LOCATION
Create Map

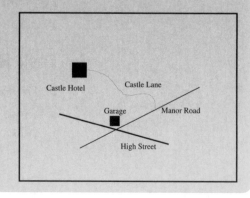

Task A

1 Read the scenario through.

2 Start the presentation software and choose a suitable template for the first slide.

3 Create the first slide, choosing a suitable font and size. Put an image of a castle at the bottom to act as a logo.

4 Create slide 2, choosing a suitable font and size for the heading and keeping the same style for all headings. Set it out with a list on the left and a suitable image on the right.

5 Create slide 3 with a heading and the text going across the slide. A suitable image should be inserted in the bottom right corner. This should be copied and reduced in size and placed in the top left corner.

6 Create slide 4 with a heading. Put an image on the left and the text on the right.

7 Create slide 5 with the heading LOCATION. Beneath this create the map.

8 Add your name as a footer.

9 Save the presentation with a suitable name.

10 Print as a handout 6 slides to a page.

11 Copy the small image on the Weddings slide and paste it into the remaining corners. Use the ruler to line up the images.

12 Copy the logo on the first page and paste it on the Location slide on both sides of the heading, changing the size if necessary.

13 Insert a new slide blank after the title slide with the following text spread across the slide. Insert the photographic image above the text.

   The Castle Hotel was opened 15 years ago and is proud of its reputation for fine service under the management of Franco Silva and his team. We have several conference and banqueting suites and can accommodate group sizes ranging from 6 to 200. We can cater for simple refreshments or a sumptuous banquet.

14 Move the slide with the map to become the second slide.

15 Change the Castle Lane line on the map to a broken line and the High Street to a heavier (thicker) line.

16 Save the presentation with a new version name.

17 Print as a handout 6 to a page.

18 Print the map slide as a single full-page slide.

Task B

1 Demonstrate to your tutor how you would group the map to make one object.

2 Demonstrate to your tutor how you would use Slide Sorter view to copy the first slide to the end of the presentation.

3 Save a new version of the presentation.

4 Print as handouts 4 to a page.

5 Show your tutor the filenames you have used.

6 Hand in all printouts.

Solutions

Section 1 Getting started

Practise your skills 1

Portway Homes	Current locations	House types
Builders of Fine Homes	• Wheatcroft • Riverside Farm • Livingstone Park • Thames Way	• 1 bedroom apartments • 2 bedroom houses • 3 bedroom semi-detached houses • 4 bedroom executive detached houses

Practise your skills 2

Greenfingers	Suppliers of	Garden Supplies
Garden Centre	• Bedding Plants • Perennials • Shrubs • Specimen trees • House plants	• Peat • Potting Compost • Fertilizer • Eco-friendly pesticides

Check your knowledge

1 A slide.

2 Outline, Slide and Notes.

3 Use a name that reflects the content.

4 Placeholders are automatically displayed on new slides ready for you to enter text, graphics or other objects. Placeholders do not show in your final presentation nor do they print.

5 Slide AutoLayouts are actually templates that help you set out the presentation in a consistent manner. There are many to choose from and they display placeholders for objects such as titles with pre-determined sizes for text. Any such template saves you time as you do not have to create each slide from scratch.

6 Bullet points are used to itemise a list of key points.

Section 2 Editing text

Practise your skills 1

Portway Homes

Builders of Quality Homes

Current locations

- Wheatcroft
- Riverside Court
- Livingstone Park
- Ridgeway Farm
- Thames Way

Home types

- 1 bedroom apartments
- 2 bedroom houses
- 3 bedroom semi-detached houses
- 4 bedroom executive detached houses

Practise your skills 2

Working with Computers

Health and Safety Issues

Everyday Problem Areas

- Eye strain
- Muscular strain
- Repetitive Strain Injury (RSI)

Check your knowledge

1 Save your work every ten minutes in case a system error or power failure occurs. You would then only lose work up to your last save.
2 The spellcheck does not spot words that are correctly spelt but used in the wrong context, e.g. I am going <u>four</u> a walk. It does not check for sense or meaning.
3 Open existing presentation.
4 Save a presentation.
5 Slide and Outline.

Section 3 Formatting text

Practise your skills 1

Portway Homes

Builders of Quality Homes

Rosemarie Wyatt

Current locations

- Wheatcroft
- Riverside Court
- Livingstone Park
- Ridgeway Farm
- Thames Way

Rosemarie Wyatt

Home types

- 1 bedroom apartments
- 2 bedroom houses
- 3 bedroom semi-detached houses
- 4 bedroom executive detached houses

Rosemarie Wyatt

Practise your skills 2

Working with Computers

Health and Safety Issues

Rosemarie Wyatt

Everyday Problem Areas

- Eye strain
- Muscular strain
- Repetitive Strain Injury (RSI)

Rosemarie Wyatt

Check your knowledge

1 Double click on the word.
2 Highlighted.
3 To change the appearance of text. It includes choice of font, size, style, emphasis and alignment.
4 Serif fonts have strokes at the ends of characters. Sans serif fonts do not.
5 Check your list against the Text presentation list on page 18.
6 To save a file by another name keeping the original intact. Often used for saving different versions of a file, e.g. Sales presentation 2.
7 Bold, italics, underline or shadow.

Consolidation 1

Printout 1

Dashwood House

Family Hotel

<small>Rosemarie Wyatt</small>

Facilities

- 24 En-suite Bedrooms
- Bar and Restaurant
- Games Room
- Swimming Pool
- Residents Lounge
- Satellite TV

<small>Rosemarie Wyatt</small>

Child-Friendly Facilities

- Children's Playroom
- Video Library
- Baby Listening Service
- Family Rooms
- Laundry

<small>Rosemarie Wyatt</small>

Printout 2

Dashwood House

Family Hotel

<small>Rosemarie Wyatt</small>

Facilities

- *24 En-suite Bedrooms*
- *Bar and Restaurant*
- *Games Room*
- *Swimming Pool*
- *Residents Lounge*
- *Satellite TV*

<small>Rosemarie Wyatt</small>

Child Friendly Facilities

- *Children's Playroom*
- *Video Library*
- *Baby Listening Service*
- *Family Rooms*
- *Laundry*

<small>Rosemarie Wyatt</small>

Section 4 Working with graphical images

Practise your skills 1

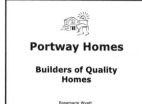

Portway Homes

Builders of Quality Homes

Rosemarie Wyatt

Current locations

- Wheatcroft
- Riverside Court
- Livingstone Park
- Ridgeway Farm
- Thames Way

Rosemarie Wyatt

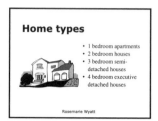

Home types

- 1 bedroom apartments
- 2 bedroom houses
- 3 bedroom semi-detached houses
- 4 bedroom executive detached houses

Rosemarie Wyatt

Practise your skills 2

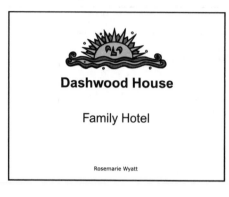

Dashwood House

Family Hotel

Rosemarie Wyatt

Facilities

- *24 En-suite Bedrooms*
- *Bar and Restaurant*
- *Games Room*
- *Swimming Pool*
- *Residents Lounge*
- *Satellite TV*

Rosemarie Wyatt

Child-Friendly Facilities

- *Children's Playroom*
- *Video Library*
- *Baby Listening Service*
- *Family Rooms*
- *Laundry*

Rosemarie Wyatt

Check your knowledge

1 Position pointer over a corner handle – pointer changes to a diagonal double-headed arrow – and drag inwards or outwards.
2 Make sure you use a corner handle.
3 A file extension is the second part of a filename added by the program used, that shows the type of file, e.g. .doc (Word file), .ppt (PowerPoint file).
4 Select Common Tasks and then Slide Layout.
5 Moving an object.
6 Move objects by selecting and dragging, or by selecting and pressing one of the four arrow keys on the keyboard.

Section 5 Running a slideshow and selecting print options

Check your knowledge

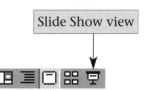
Slide Show view

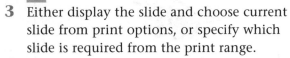

1   **Esc** key is the Escape key and will stop a slideshow in progress.

2

3   Either display the slide and choose current slide from print options, or specify which slide is required from the print range.

4   The slides have lines alongside with space for writing notes.

Consolidation 2

Version 1

Pointer Devices

Rosemarie Wyatt

Mouse

- Move the mouse across the desk to move pointer
- Press button to click and select
- Sometimes have a scroll wheel
- Most common device

Rosemarie Wyatt

Touchpad

- Available on laptop computers
- Small, sensitive pads
- Move finger across to move pointer
- Tap the pad to click and select

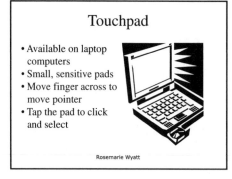

Rosemarie Wyatt

Trackball

- A mouse lying on its back
- Rotate the ball to move the pointer
- Tap buttons either side of ball to click

Rosemarie Wyatt

Version 2

Pointer Devices

Rosemarie Wyatt

Mouse

- Move the mouse across the desk to move pointer
- Press button to click and select
- Sometimes have a scroll wheel
- Most common device

Rosemarie Wyatt

Touchpad

- Available on laptop computers
- Small, sensitive pads
- Move finger across to move pointer
- Tap the pad to click and select

Rosemarie Wyatt

Trackball

- A mouse lying on its back
- Rotate the ball to move the pointer
- Tap buttons either side of ball to click

Rosemarie Wyatt

Section 6 Creating and modifying graphical objects

Practise your skills 1 and 2

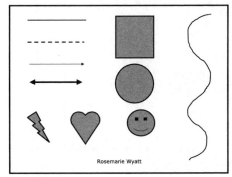

Version 1

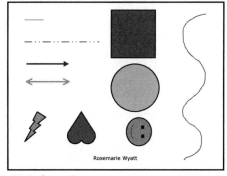

Version 2

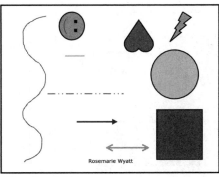

Version 3

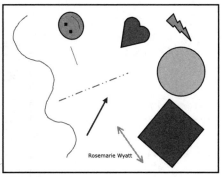

Version 4

Check your knowledge

1 Flip it horizontally.
2 An object that has been flipped vertically or turned upside down.
3 Hold down the shift key when using the oval tool.
4 A handle.
5 Drag on the line around the edge.

Section 7 Manipulating graphical objects

Practise your skills 1

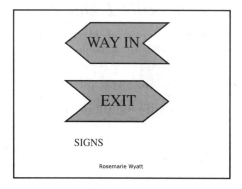

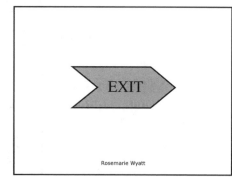

Practise your skills 2

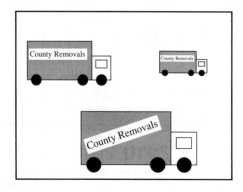

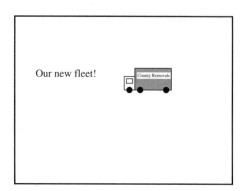

Check your knowledge

1 When you use copy or cut, clipboard is the area of memory where the information is held until you **paste** it where required.
2 It will move back one layer and end up in between the other two layers.
3 Hold down the shift key and click each object in turn.
4 Drag on the edge.
5 Select one of the previously grouped objects and click on **Draw – Regroup**.

Consolidation 3

Printout 1

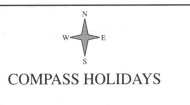

COMPASS HOLIDAYS

Faraway destinations

WHAT WE OFFER

- Escorted tours
- Experienced Guides
- Tried and tested destinations
- Recommended Hotels

FEATURES OF OUR TOURS

- Transport from your front door
- Constant tour guide supervision
- Two guides for each tour
- No surcharge for singles
- Group bookings a speciality

CURRENT DESTINATIONS

- India
- Australia
- South Africa
- China

Printout 2

CURRENT DESTINATIONS

- India
- Australia
- South Africa
- China

Section 8 Further editing and layout

Practise your skills 1 and 2

Tour Guide Experience

Our guides have many years travel experience between them and much local knowledge to give you the very best taste of the region you have chosen to travel to.

Guide	Experience
John Kempson	10 years
Marcella Martinez	15 years
Haizhu Lee	12 years
David Wells	15 years

Languages spoken

- Haizhu Lee
  - Mandarin
  - Cantonese
- John Kempson
  - Hindi
  - Panjabi

Check your knowledge

1 Indents make text in a paragraph stand out from the rest of the text. They are also used to indent bullets making them sub-bullets of the main bullet points.
2 Copy it from the original application and paste it onto a slide.
3 To set out text and numbers lined up in columns.
4 Landscape – wide edge at the top.
5 Click on the bottom of the ruler at the point required.

Section 9 Organising slides

Practise your skills 1

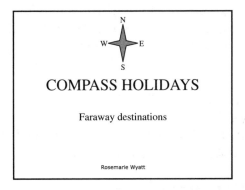

COMPASS HOLIDAYS

Faraway destinations

Rosemarie Wyatt

FEATURES OF OUR TOURS

- Transport from your front door
- Constant tour guide supervision
- Two guides for each tour
- No surcharge for singles
- Group bookings a speciality

Rosemarie Wyatt

CURRENT DESTINATIONS

- India
- Australia
- South Africa
- China

Rosemarie Wyatt

NEXT DEPARTURES

India	March
China	April
South Africa	June
Australia	September

Rosemarie Wyatt

WHAT WE OFFER

- Escorted tours
- Experienced Guides
- Tried and tested destinations
- Recommended Hotels

Rosemarie Wyatt

COMPASS HOLIDAYS

Faraway destinations

Rosemarie Wyatt

Check your knowledge

1 In Slide Sorter view, select a slide and press **Delete** on the keyboard. You can also do this in the Outline pane.
2 In Slide Sorter view, select a slide, click on **Copy**. Click between slides in required position and click on **Paste**. You can also do this in the Outline pane.
3 In Slide Sorter view, select a slide and drag to its new position. You can also do this in the Outline pane.
4 You might want to repeat the title slide at the end of a show to reinforce the title. You might also want to use a slide as the basis for a new slide.

Section 10 Hardware considerations

Check your knowledge

1 The highest you can – currently 2 GHz.
2 The highest you can – currently around 256 Mb.
3 The largest on offer. The standard size is currently 17″, 19″ is even better.
4 A laptop computer and a projector.
5 Floppy disk and CD.
6 Laser.
7 Printed colour does not always match what you see onscreen. Colour-coded drawings or diagrams will not show up clearly, if at all.

Practice assignments

Practice assignment 1

Printout 1

Health and Safety

Working with Computers

Rosemarie Wyatt

Office Chairs

• Adjustable height
• Adjustable backs
• Swivel seats
• Wheels

Rosemarie Wyatt

Computer Screens

• Tiltable screens
• Flicker-free
• Non-reflective
• Position to avoid glare from windows

Rosemarie Wyatt

Eye Strain

This can be a problem and staff should be encouraged to rest their eyes frequently and focus away from the screen from time to time. We can provide screen filters if requested. Please ensure blinds are in use at all windows

Rosemarie Wyatt

Repetitive Strain Injury

This is otherwise known as RSI and is caused by frequent wrist movement and poor posture. We provide wrist rests and staff must be encouraged to use them. Please ensure staff are aware of the dangers of RSI

Rosemarie Wyatt

Reporting procedure

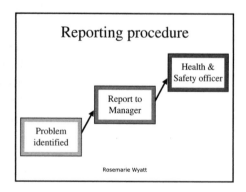

Problem identified → Report to Manager → Health & Safety officer

Rosemarie Wyatt

Printout 2

Health and Safety

Working with Computers

Rosemarie Wyatt

Reporting procedure

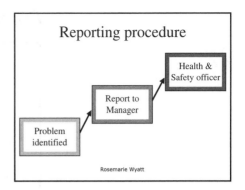

Rosemarie Wyatt

Office Chairs

- Adjustable height
- Adjustable backs
- Swivel seats
- Wheels

Rosemarie Wyatt

Computer Screens

- Tiltable screens
- Flicker-free
- Non-reflective
  - Position to avoid glare from windows

Rosemarie Wyatt

Eye Strain

This can be a problem and staff should be encouraged to rest their eyes frequently and focus away from the screen from time to time. We can provide screen filters if requested. Please ensure blinds are in use at all windows

Rosemarie Wyatt

Repetitive Strain Injury

This is otherwise known as RSI and is caused by frequent wrist movement and poor posture. We provide wrist rests and staff must be encouraged to use them. Please ensure staff are aware of the dangers of RSI

Rosemarie Wyatt

Practice assignment 2
Printout 1

CASTLE HOTEL AND
CONFERENCE CENTRE

Conferences and Weddings

Rosemarie Wyatt

CONFERENCES

- Fully serviced conferences for up to 200
- Gourmet catering
- Special overnight accomodation rates
- Regular customer discounts

Rosemarie Wyatt

 WEDDINGS

- Weddings luncheons, buffets and dinners
- Cordon Bleu cuisine
- Flowers
- Music
- Special overnight rates for guests

Rosemarie Wyatt

CATERING SERVICES

- Silver Service
- Hot or cold buffet
- Finger buffet
- Refreshments

Rosemarie Wyatt

LOCATION

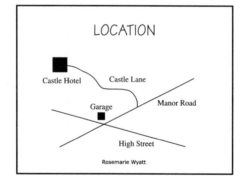

Castle Hotel   Castle Lane

Garage   Manor Road

High Street

Rosemarie Wyatt

Printout 2

CASTLE HOTEL AND
CONFERENCE CENTRE

Conferences and Weddings

Rosemarie Wyatt

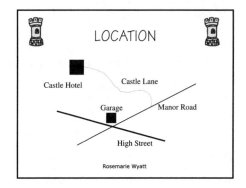

LOCATION

Castle Hotel · Castle Lane · Garage · Manor Road · High Street

Rosemarie Wyatt

The Castle Hotel was opened 15 years ago and is proud of its reputation for fine service under the management of Franco Silva and his team. We have several conference and banqueting suites and can accomodate group sizes ranging from 6 to 200. We can cater for simple refreshments or a sumptuous banquet

Rosemarie Wyatt

CONFERENCES

- Fully serviced conferences for up to 200
- Gourmet catering
- Special overnight accomodation rates
- Regular customer discounts

Rosemarie Wyatt

WEDDINGS

- Weddings luncheons, buffets and dinners
- Cordon Bleu cuisine
- Flowers
- Music
- Special overnight rates for guests

Rosemarie Wyatt

CATERING SERVICES

- Silver Service
- Hot or cold buffet
- Finger buffet
- Refreshments

Rosemarie Wyatt

Printout 3

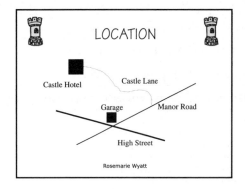

LOCATION

Castle Hotel · Castle Lane · Garage · Manor Road · High Street

Rosemarie Wyatt

Outcomes matching guide

Outcome 1 Create and edit presentations graphics

Practical activities

1	Load presentation graphics software	Section 1
2	Open an existing template and add text	Section – All
3	Import selected text from other applications	Section 8
4	Use a spellchecker	Section 2
5	Resize text and change font attributes	Section 3
6	Use indented and bulleted text	Section – All
7	Use systematic filenames	Sections 2–9

Underpinning knowledge

1	Identify the hardware requirements for use of a presentation graphics software package: • Processor power and memory requirements	Section 10
2	Identify the advantages of using templates	Section 1
3	Identify the special features which attractively present text to suit a defined purpose: text size, text attributes, use of space, indentation, bullets	Sections 3, 8

Outcome 2 Create and edit presentation graphics

Practical activities

1	Insert clip art from disk or network drive or from CD, Internet	Sections 4–9
2	From a file insert a graphical object • Bitmap • Compressed photo or scanned graphic • Compress drawn graphic	Section 4
3	Place and resize object in the page	Section 9
4	Duplicate and delete object, copy object to another page	Section 7
5	Insert pre-defined shapes and add additional lines and arrows	Section 6
6	Add text to a pre-defined shape	Section 7
7	Modify colour and lines for a pre-defined shape	Section 6
8	Group a set of graphical objects	Section 7

Outcome 3 Position and manipulate text and graphics

Practical activities

1	Set page margins, tabs and indents	Section 8
2	Place text next to a graphical object	Section 7
3	Position and align text and graphical objects using the ruler	Section 7
4	Group text with a graphical object	Section 7
5	Reposition and resize grouped objects	Section 7
6	Use layers to order objects	Section 7
7	Rotate, mirror and invert objects	Section 6

Outcome 4 Create, print and demonstrate a multi-slide show		
Practical activities		
1	Create a new multi-slide show	Sections – All
2	Duplicate and delete slides	Section 9
3	View and reorder slides	Section 9
4	Run the slideshow	Sections 5–9
5	Use a pointer device to control slide transition	Sections 5–9
6	Print a single slide from the presentation	Section 5
7	Print the whole presentation as a handout	Sections 5–9
8	Close the presentation graphics software	Sections – All
Underpinning knowledge		
1	Identify the hardware requirements for presenting a slide show: ● Display type (large monitor, projector) and resolution ● Portable storage medium ● Printer type (Colour/monochrome; Laser/inkjet) and resolution ● Pointer device	Section 10 Section 5
2	Identify the problems associated with printing colour slides using a monochrome printer	Sections 6, 10

Quick reference guide

Action	Button	Menu	Keyboard
Bold	**B**	Format – Font	Ctrl + B
Bullets	≔	Format – Bullets and Numbering	
Cancel			Esc
Centre align	≡	Format – Alignment	Ctrl + E
Change case		Format – Change case	
Change slide layout	Common Tasks ▾ / New Slide... Ctrl+M / Slide Layout... / Apply Design Template...	Format – Slide Layout	
Close or Exit		File – Close or Exit	Alt + F4
Copy		Edit – Copy	Ctrl + C
Copy a slide	In Slide Sorter view – select slide – Copy – paste in new position or Insert – duplicate slide		
Cut	✂	Edit – Cut	Ctrl + X
Demote (Indent)	➡		
End of line			End
Exit or Close		File – Close or Exit	Alt + F4
Font	Arial ▾	Format – Font	
Font size	10 ▾	Format – Font	
Footer		View – Header and Footer	
Group		Draw toolbar – Draw – Group	
Indent (Demote)	➡		
Insert clip art	🖼 From Drawing toolbar	Insert – Picture – ClipArt	
Insert new slide		Insert – New Slide	
Insert picture		Insert – Picture – From File	
Italics	*I*	Format – Font	Ctrl + I
Justify	≣	Format – Alignment	Ctrl + J
Left align	≣	Format – Alignment	Ctrl + L
Line spacing		Format – Line spacing	

New presentation		File – New	Ctrl + N
New slide		Insert – New Slide	
Normal view		View – Normal	
Numbering		Format – Bullets and Numbering	
Open file		File – Open	Ctrl + O
Paper size/orientation		File – Page Setup	
Paste		Edit – Paste	Ctrl + V
Print		File – Print	Ctrl + P
Promote			
Redo		Edit – Redo	
Right align		Format – Alignment	Ctrl + R
Ruler		View – Ruler	
Save		File – Save	Ctrl + S
Save as		File – Save As	F12
Select all (in a text box)		Edit – Select All	Ctrl + A
Shadow		Format – Font	
Slide order (change)	In Slide Sorter view – drag slide to new position In Outline pane – drag slide icon to new position		
Slide Show view		View – Slide Show	F5
Slide Sorter view		View – Slide Sorter	
Slide view			
Spellcheck		Tools – Spelling and Grammar	F7
Start of line			Home
Text box		Insert – text box	
Underline		Format – Font	Ctrl + U
Undo		Edit – Undo	
Ungroup		Drawing toolbar – Draw – Ungroup	
View options		View menu – Select (except Slide view)	

Select text

To select:	Method
One word	Double click on word (also selects the following space)
Several words	Press and drag the I-beam across several words and release
A sentence	Hold down **Ctrl**. Click anywhere in sentence
A block of text	Click cursor at start point, hold down **Shift**. Click cursor at end point.
To deselect	Click anywhere off the text

Right mouse button

Clicking the right mouse button provides menu options depending on what you are doing at the time, e.g. when right clicked in text, you have Cut, Copy, Paste, etc.

Drawing toolbar

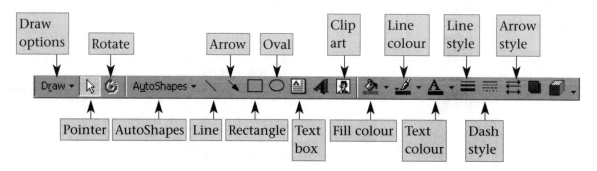